What people are sayin.

WanderLOST

The Scripture says that we work out our salvation with fear and trembling. It's not about a moment... it's about a movement of the Spirit in us. *WanderLOST* is a beautiful story, a tremendous-global-adventure kind of story, of one man's salvation being worked out with fear and trembling. Sims asks all the right questions. He gently invites you to ask them with him. He travels the world and brings you along. He offers the hope he has found with a humility that invites you to ponder with him where you have found hope. This is one wanderer sharing with the rest of us where he found home. One hungry traveler telling us where we can find food. One young man in the wilderness telling us where there is a source of good water.
Shane Claiborne, Activist, Author, founder – The Simple Way

WanderLOST ushers the reader into an authentic adventure – gently asking questions along the way while pointing us toward hope and sustenance for the journey. Through the years, Sims has proven himself to be a strategic thinker, committed to relationships... innovative and ever-willing to grow himself as a leader and follower of Christ. These qualities are evident throughout *WanderLOST*. I appreciate all that was poured into this story and trust there will be many who benefit from both his candor and humility.
Gary Haugen, Founder/CEO – International Justice Mission

WanderLOST is a story about one man's outer adventures and inner journey, but it is also a story which gets at the very core of what it means to be human. As Aleksandr Solzhenitsyn stated, "The battleline between good and evil runs through the heart of every man." As a key component of this battle, Sims boldly confronts our modern understanding of what it really means to be free. In doing so, he asks us to question those things in our lives which keep us from reaching for that deeper freedom which can only emerge from a right relationship with our Creator. This is a story which asks us to recognize our own finiteness and insufficiency to do anything beyond radically loving those "others" placed in our midst. This is the best kind of story, not just because it is interesting and relatable, but because it is true. **David Eubank**, Founder/CEO – Free Burma Rangers

In *WanderLOST*, Sims tells a globe-spanning story of a young man's search for a life that counts for something. It's his own story, recounted with an appealing vulnerability and straightforwardness, and it takes us to places as varied as the Middle East, West and East Africa, Latin America, Southeast Asia, and the United States. Through telling a wide range of experiences, this story forces the reader to grapple with fundamental human questions: What is freedom, and what is justice? What gives purpose to life? And what does it mean to surrender to this purpose? For anyone like Sims who, through his international work for human rights and development, has been immersed in the realities of how much of humanity lives, these questions are anything but theoretical. Nor should they be for the rest of us in a deeply interconnected world.
Peter Mommsen, Editor-in-Chief, *Plough Quarterly*

J. Daniel Sims is the kind of storyteller thinking travelers want to hear from. In *WanderLOST*, he offers the kind of deeply insightful and timely message which can only be born out of an adventurous life. Yet, he is also suitably vulnerable – flawed, self-aware, funny, torn by true love – you know, just the guy to make the hours fly by in any bug-eaten corner of the world. What's more, he offers a convicting account of how easily us

Western travelers can despoil the places and cultures we come home raving about. Through his immersive storytelling and trenchant observations, Sims will keep you turning pages all night under your mosquito net. *WanderLOST* broke my heart and shone a ray of hope. I highly recommend it.
David Kopp, Founding Editor, Convergent Books, Penguin Random House

In *WanderLOST*, Sims tells a story that is so particular it becomes universal, especially for the traveler or the globally minded Christ-follower. But anyone who has searched for meaning, identity, or community will find in him a fellow seeker. At times hilarious and at times heartbreaking, *WanderLOST* is at all times compelling.
Elizabeth Trotter, Executive Editor, A Life Overseas

WanderLOST is a reflective tale of adventure and spiritual growth so honest that it critiques its own motives and the very essence of adventure itself. Having taken the ideals of young adventurous American life to their extreme ends, Sims offers a well-articulated contemplation of the shortcomings of such a life. He has a unique way of penetrating right through a story to reveal its depth of importance and pinpoint the greater meaning, underlying motive, etc. I found myself applying his takeaways to my own similar experiences and tearing up at his revelations and fresh interpretation. In sum, it is a book you can't put down but also can't resist processing the implications as you go.
Brant Copen, Executive Director – AIM, India

Mr. Sims, thank you for your kind and interesting note. Sadly, I currently lack the time to make honest work of review writing. Thus, I am honored by your request but must humbly decline. Yours sincerely.
Wendell Berry, Novelist, Poet, Essayist, Activist, Farmer

WanderLOST

stories from the winding road
toward significance

WanderLOST

stories from the winding road
toward significance

J. Daniel Sims

**CIRCLE
BOOKS**

Winchester, UK
Washington, USA

JOHN HUNT PUBLISHING

First published by Circle Books, 2023
Circle Books is an imprint of John Hunt Publishing Ltd., No. 3 East St., Alresford,
Hampshire SO24 9EE, UK
office@jhpbooks.com
www.johnhuntpublishing.com
www.circle-books.com

For distributor details and how to order please visit the 'Ordering' section on our website.

ISBN: 978 1 78535 977 4
978 1 78535 978 1 (ebook)
Library of Congress Control Number: 2021949994

A CIP catalogue record for this book is available from the British Library.

Design: Stuart Davies

UK: Printed and bound by CPI Group (UK) Ltd, Croydon, CR0 4YY
US: Printed and bound by Thomson Shore, 7300 West Joy Road, Dexter, MI 48130

We operate a distinctive and ethical publishing philosophy in
all areas of our business, from our global network of authors to
production and worldwide distribution.

Contents

In *Finite and Infinite Games*, James P. Carse states enigmatically, "If we cannot tell a story about what happened to us, nothing has happened to us."
This book tells a story about what happened to me.
It is dedicated to my dear friend Jeremy Shull – whose own story was so beautifully told that it spoke truth into my life.

The man with the clear head is the man who... looks life in the face, realizes that everything in it is problematic, and feels himself lost. And this is the simple truth — that to live is to feel oneself lost — he who accepts it has already begun to find himself, to be on firm ground. Instinctively, as do the shipwrecked, he will look round for something to which to cling, and that tragic, ruthless glance, absolutely sincere, because it is a question of his salvation, will begin to bring order into the chaos of his life. These are the only genuine ideas; the ideas of the shipwrecked. All the rest is rhetoric, posturing, farce. He who does not really feel himself lost, is without remission; that is to say, he never finds himself, never comes up against reality.

Jose Ortega y Gasset

Section 1

The wind in my face

Chapter 1

There is nothing quite like looking, if you want to find something. You certainly usually find something, if you look, but it is not always quite the something you were after.
J.R.R. Tolkien, The Hobbit

The aging Toyota Hilux jolts, groans, and surges forward as it slams roughly into third. It is in this moment when the *magic* hits. Physically, today, the *magic* takes the form of a thousand million bits of sand, the warm, rich odor of petrol smacking me in the face as I squint and grin into the rising sun and soft wind of a picturesque Arabian desert.

The simple physicality of this moment is not fully pleasant in its own right. The sun is just a bit too bright. The sand burns a little and gets caught up in my teeth; the truck heaves and lurches across uneven terrain. The roll bar along the back of the cab is rust-rough. In spite of the mild discomfort and slight risk of tetanus, gripping it tightly is a must in order to remain upright.

The physical sensations aren't all bad, though. The ever-changing portrait steals breath away, revealing itself as the canyon yawns open to a sea of dunes and rock features. It is novel and stunning and unlike anything you might stumble across in "normal" American life. At this moment, the temperature is just right. The sun brings warmth as much as glare to the cool desert morning. The bumps in this road are over soft sand as we hurtle deeper into the desert sun and growing wind.

Yet this moment, this *magic*, is so much more than the physical sensations which define it. The possibilities are endless as the wind races through hair and skin and lungs in the back of a speeding truck.

The feeling is hard to pin down. Yet, it is central – the

intangible inner core of that thing driving me and others like me ever onward.

Fear is certainly a part of it, an initial reaction to such experiences. Clinging tightly to the decaying roll bar of an aging truck at speeds approaching reckless on "roads" of less than DOT-approved minimum grade is a bit unsettling, to be sure. For the rational, grounded rider, this is the moment where you think back to your single interaction with the driver and wonder whether he is indeed old enough to be qualified for this task.

And perhaps, as he continues his rough-handed assault through the gears – flying now over hills, around curves – your stomach starts to turn with uncertainty as much as nausea. Maybe that's where it ends for you. You hop out at your destination, decide "enough is enough," and thank God you lived to tell the tale.

However, for me, and perhaps many others of my ilk, fear is only the beginning. We are on a frenzied metaphysical quest which transcends the rational, a lost and wandering hunt for some abstract "ultimate" ideal. We are straining beyond reason – beyond reality itself – toward the mirage of becoming something new, something other than our finite selves through these moments of wind coursing through hair and lungs.

And what is fear in the face of such a grand, self-actualizing adventure? It is but one in an endless sea of barriers as we yearn for a glimpse of the deeper longings, ethereal urges driving us deeper into this desert and others.

Chapter 2

When I was very young and the urge to be someplace else was on me, I was assured by mature people that maturity would cure this itch. When years described me as mature, the remedy prescribed was middle age. In middle age I was assured that greater age would calm my fever and now that I am fifty-eight perhaps senility will do the job. Nothing has worked.
John Steinbeck, Travels with Charley in Search of America

My first glimpse of these ethereal urges came from the back of another truck, this time an oxidizing Ford, flying across a wide patch of West Texas clay.

I was 4 years old and propped up on the decaying roll bar in my dad's arms. Looking back now, the driver's age and skills weren't in question. Though I doubt Jose had a license.

In fact, it would be another decade before Jose grasped in his hands so much as a documented right to work on this patch of clay. But immigration status hadn't stopped him from becoming part of my family or moving his own north to Pappaw's farm. Jose skillfully managed the land and, by our reckoning at least, had found a better life here.

As we tear across the pasture – the wind lifting me above the lowly plains and particularities of mere childhood – an indescribable feeling overtakes me.

In my mind, nothing holds me back – though my father's strong arms certainly do.

In my heart, the possibilities are infinite and all doors open – the limiting reality of life and the choices I must make are not yet clear.

In my soul, mine is a globally shared experience – the isolating nature of my biases and blind spots remain obscured.

I do not yet realize it, but in this moment, I am, in fact, at *the pinnacle.* In the grand story of humanity, my material advantages are unprecedented. I am privileged, precocious, healthy, white and male. I am wrapped in the embrace of a loving family. This family has been supported, propelled, lifted for generations by the sweat, ingenuity, and tireless good humor of other cultures both seen and unseen.

And *the pinnacle* is more than mere birthright. It is also that intangible core, that unarticulated urge, that whisper of something yet to be attained.

The racing tires and these strong arms and the wind in my face encourage me in language I can't yet fully process, but know deeply as a simple fact. For me, in this moment, as much as any time or place in history, the possibilities to transcend and achieve and conquer and explore are indeed endless. This "truth" is so real to me it almost screams as a universal.

What I feel, what I know, what I am offered in this moment amongst countless others through the coming decades is a uniquely *American* dream.

This otherworldly illusion is a phenomenon and a feeling and an essence which guides and pushes and puffs us modern, wealthy, westerners up at every turn. A concept whose true meaning we've turned and twisted and all but forgotten, but which drives us forward across plains and deserts, and oceans and mountains, and patches of west Texas clay with a ferocity and ease never before seen.

In a word – freedom.

Chapter 3

I sensed there was a great difference between unfettered personal license and real freedom.
Bruce Springsteen

My mind darts back from this early Texas memory, through the intervening three decades of wind and truck rides and freedom unbridled across six continents and well over 70 countries, to today's little adventure. Here, in the back of this truck in Wadi Rum, Jordan, I am driven by the same urges. Yet, the empty promise of a lifetime at the *pinnacle* of human history is driving cracks in my understanding of it all.

More than anything, mine is a story about these "cracks." It is about the non-linear, often unconscious project of learning that you don't have all the answers. It is about the gradual acceptance that everything in life is problematic; that you will never learn how to put all the pieces together. It is about the humility which dawns as you realize the depth of your ignorance runs far deeper than you can ever hope to fully grasp. It's about wrestling with the tension of knowing you must continue to try.

The *pinnacle*, to me, embodies just such a "crack," a poorly understood but deeply felt moment for a fortunate few. From this pinnacle, *we* overlook while lacking the eyes to truly see the deep cracks and crevices – the oppressive history which brought *us* to this summit. And, as *our* place at the pinnacle blinds *us* to the reality below, it also fills, lifts, and often crushes *us* with the vast potential and perceived mandate to summit and conquer anew; to customize *our* lives; to choose.

Choice is an idol for many in the ascendent demographic of my generation, and we choose like none before us – imagining ourselves free and dislocated from the chains and constraints of the past, of our own histories, of reality itself.

Each of us grasps, to varying degrees, the gravity of this moment. Each of us responds to this call to choose in our own way.

Yet, this trend, this worship of choice, extends beyond the wealthy and beyond the millennial generation. Traces of it are found throughout our broader culture. Regardless of the political identity or topic of discussion, modern Americans love throwing around terms like "freedom," "rights," and "liberty." Whether we're right, left, or center, so much of our worlds are consumed and defined by these concepts. Our underlying assumptions about "freedom" get elevated to the status of culturally accepted truths as the cracks lie willfully disregarded below.

But what does that word "freedom" even mean?

If you asked me what freedom meant a few years back, you would probably hear some variant of the word "choice" or "possibility." To me, freedom meant the option to pick and do what I wanted, to customize my life how I saw fit. Freedom meant to live uninhibited by the burden of being told what to do by another, to exist autonomously, and to be liberated from the obligation of being tied to a given thing.

I hunted this mirage of freedom through travel – via truck rides and flights and jostling informal buses – to the world's great luxury resorts, deserted beaches, bustling cities, small quaint villages, and gorgeous mountain passes.

I sought liberty via vocational pursuit – taking advantage of this odd moment in history where a small number are privileged by the opportunity to align careers closely with skills, interests, and maybe even passions.

I deified choice in pursuit of niche expertise verging on snobbery each time I fancied myself a budding connoisseur of single origin coffee, local craft beer, organic kale, kombucha, or kimchi.

I fumbled for individuality and self-definition by customizing my life via the American Gold Standard of material acquisition – buying continuously more and better cars, homes, clothes and the like. Yet it was not always in the acquisition itself, but in the customization of those things acquired – curating, designing my home, possessions and virtual life – that I developed a sense of self I wished to portray to the world.

I dreamt of this "freedom" only semi-consciously at times but always buffered by the historical blanket of violent systems of power and privilege. These systems – built by the various, insidious techniques of the modern world – offer a "crack" blinded material prosperity to people like me while smothering the aspirations of billions of faceless others.

As I reflect on this lost, wandering excuse for a life story, I am constantly confronted by the enormous volume of time and energy I and others around me devote to our disembodied visions of self. In this moment, at *the pinnacle*, we are consumed, driven, and blinded by our superficial choices as the world groans under the weight of our cherished "freedom."

Chapter 4

There are no unsacred places; there are only sacred places and desecrated places.
Wendell Berry, Given

The sky is stark blue, cloudless; the landscape enormous and uniform. The wind and the jolts of the truck's momentum are the only real indicators that we are in motion.

As I try and fail to grasp the novelty and grandeur of this moment, I silently wonder to myself. *Is this it? Have I now attained this "thing" we call "freedom"? If not, if it is more slippery than something you can grasp via experience or acquisition, then what am I seeking here, racing across the desert?*

And what is it that drives these others sitting beside me?

That's right. It is not just me in the back of this aging Toyota Hilux, romantically imagining and realizing conquest of an exotic, virgin desert landscape. There are eight others crammed in this truck bed with me. Perhaps I forgot about them as I stood, blocking their view, their moment in the sun, their time to pretend they are truly exploring with the wind in their faces.

Perhaps, I forgot about them because I have blinders on. I have been running headlong in focused pursuit of such experiences for so long. For a solid decade, I've been on and off the road, racking up explorations and stories and pictures and countries.

Sometimes these "others" are visibly with me on the adventure. Increasingly, their presence is obscured by the deceptive veils of space and time as my yearnings take me further and further from the "beaten path." To be clear though, mine is not an uncommon quest. Regardless of whether I see them or not, I am not alone in this adventure.

That is just not how life works, particularly in our globalized, interconnected, twenty-first-century existence. This is not an individual adventure; nothing really is.

The story of tourism, viewed honestly, is a cultural conquest.

* * *

The place and people of Wadi Rum know this story as well as most. This desert valley was a former outpost of the Roman and Ottoman Empires and later a colonial territory of the once expansive British Empire. The Bedouin people of Wadi Rum – split today by an arbitrary border between Jordan and Saudi Arabia – now face perhaps the greatest challenge yet to their way of life.

Each day, dozens of trucks just like mine roll through the once desolate hills and dunes. These trucks bring tourists eager to take their small piece of this history and land which once stood remote, apart.

And this time, the conquest, the betrayal is deeper. It is led by the Wadi's own people – fueled by the money pouring in and the promise of what those resources might bring, but never do. Tour by tour, day by day, they trade an old way of life for the fragmentation and false promises of a world beyond.

* * *

As I wrap up my token camel ride around the quintessentially Instagram-perfect desert landscape, I realize I've seen it one too many times. I don't want to be part of *this* story for *these* people any longer.

To this tragedy amongst others, I view myself now as fully "woke" – even though I am certainly far from it; even if the cracks are so deep I can't fully see what "woke" really means; even if "wokeness" itself is just one more label I'm hoping will carve out and validate my identity to a world I still think cares.

In the end, I may still be sleeping but my eyes are open and my stomach turns at the systems to which my choices contribute in my daily, "normal" life at home and out here on the road. Yet, all the awokeness, er, awareness in the world doesn't itself produce the character necessary to be different.

"Perhaps," I lie to myself for the millionth time, "the problem is once again here in this place. Surely, it is not with me. Maybe, a better, more 'authentic' experience will heal me and set me free from this mess."

So, with my privilege and my money and my inexplicable, unprecedented American ability to be everywhere and nowhere all at once, I hop out of this rusted old truck – into my rented SUV – and head north.

Chapter 5

Men go abroad to wonder at the heights of mountains, at the huge waves of the sea, at the long courses of the rivers, at the vast compass of the ocean, at the circular motions of the stars, and they pass by themselves without wondering.
Augustine of Hippo

A few hours later, I pull off King's Highway toward the small village of Dana and am surprised to encounter the first dirt roads of my trip. A few kilometers further and I arrive at the "visitor center"; a lean-to structure with a platform at the end, gazing out over a ridiculously beautiful valley below. Or, I should say, the skeleton of a platform. The crew hadn't deemed it necessary to include floor planks on the viewing deck which shot out 1500 feet above the yawning canyon floor.

Not fully unaware of the irony, I still can't resist a quick selfie which I'll gleefully post later.

Just down the road is Dana village, the gateway to Jordan's largest National Park. Instead of a refined industry of hip cafes and craft markets and tour guides and ticket salesmen, there are crumbling stone buildings perched along the canyon rim. A cobblestone main street with just a few aging cars leads to a single hotel with an open roof restaurant, a great view, and no other guest in sight.

For a single dinar, I grab some water and a quick chat with the proprietor. In the absence of a thousand screaming TripAdvisor reviews ranking the relative merits of the various options, the manager offers me some local guidance in the direction of a particularly good hike. I follow an 8-mile jaw-dropper around the canyon rim to the astonishing overlook at which I now stand.

* * *

Gazing out across the vast *wadi*, taking in the array of colors, the scale and physical beauty and the silence, I finally glimpse that elusive wonder which good travel always brings, but is increasingly difficult to find.

Ultimately, it is the silence – broken only by the soft chiming of a goat's bell off in the distance – which brings it home for me. The power of this silence emanates from the rare yet satisfying knowledge that another tourist is unlikely to intrude on *my* moment.

At this point, after all this travel, only when I am alone can I effectively imagine that I'm truly exploring. Silence implies that I am, for once, alone, for once, truly "free" – or, at least, truly blind to a more complete view of reality.

Arriving at this place of solace and freedom and blindness required a small bit of risk as well. Not physical, mortal risk to be sure. Jordan is a very safe country. Rather, it was the risk of stepping into a small void beyond the long arm of social opinion.

There was no such void present at the Roman Amphitheater in Amman, or the ruins of Jerash, or the Monastery at Mt. Nebo, or the lavish resorts of the Dead Sea. There was certainly no void, no risk of disappointment venturing to the "lost" city of Petra of Indiana Jones fame nor to Wadi Rum, the desert motif which birthed Lawrence of Arabia.

All these places were well reviewed, gushed over by travel bloggers and Instagram influencers, thoroughly overrun by some combination of touts and more sophisticated tourist money extractors. All were definitely worth the hype, but there was no question, no mystery as to what I'd experience in each place given the enormous digital footprints left by the most recent (predominantly millennial) wanderlusting passersby.

* * *

To be fair, Dana is not unknown. It is not truly off the beaten path. Honestly, it is still probably one of the top attractions in the country, but its fame has not yet reached the frothing, selfie-riddled apex of the others.

I also have to be honest with myself as I enjoy this moment of travel nirvana. I must be clear in this "risk" I describe. Finding this moment was not truly difficult nor did it require much in terms of "travel skill." I don't speak a word of Arabic. Because of my job, I have a basic grasp of the complex political dynamics which face this country. I know a few things about Jordan's rich history, culture, and economy. Yet prior to arrival, I had never heard of its major attractions beyond Petra. I knew no locals to serve as a guide, nor did I employ one during my 4-day weekend of travel to Petra, Wadi Rum, and Dana.

The crazy thing about my general lack of preparation is that none of it mattered because of the trail of digital footprints left behind by previous travelers.

Granted, it is a small country (about the size of Connecticut) with great roads. Nonetheless, to experience all that so painlessly with no knowledge or skill whatsoever?

Literally anyone could do this. More to the point, in a world such as ours, when things are that easy and look as attractive as this place does, then everyone from "the pinnacle" *will* do it.

For the future thriving of the particular people who hail from this land, that is a scary prospect.

* * *

As I reflect here and soak in this moment of freedom and silence and beauty, I am struck by what my heart yearns to do. *This is it. This is the dream, the goal, the apex of what travel is and should be. An impromptu decision, a village chock full of history and character, a conversation with a local to learn a bit about the place and get their advice, eyes opened to a stunning new experience and perspective.*

This moment, for me, is a perfect embodiment of that expressive individualistic mirage of freedom via exploration.

There is a significant part of me that wants to share it. In my desire for connection with others, I want them to experience this place, this feeling, this moment exactly as I do. In my desire to distinguish myself from others, I also long for it to be known that I had this experience, this moment, this conquest. In a sense, I lust credit for discovering this place; being changed by it, being better for it.

I hope to believe – and I strive for others to see – that I seek authenticity and beauty and solace in a shallow, hectic material world. I need to announce my conquest, my victory to the world, or at least those around me.

But therein lies the paradox. If I do share and post and if everyone else does as well, this place will become like all the others. The pure becomes spoiled, and we must seek the conquest anew.

In this moment, I'm comparing Dana to the Bedouin tourist paradise of Wadi Rum. But it could just as easily be any other place which combines cultural eminence with physical beauty – Macchu Pichu, the Pyramids of Giza, Mt. Kilimanjaro, the Grand Canyon, French Riviera, and Angkor Wat amongst many others.

The story is always the same.

* * *

Once upon a time, there was a group of people who lived in a specific place with a particular culture and a unique way of life.

At some point, outsiders discovered this specific place and shared the news back home. Over time, other wealthy outsiders began to find the place and its meaning significant or exotic enough to seek out experiences there.

Far, far away from the people who lived in the specific place, increasing pockets of wealth in other countries and a growing awareness by rich people of this "special exotic place" combined to bring about a new reality. In this new reality, more and more relatively wealthy outsiders were able to experience this particular place and pay its people a pittance for that experience. As they did, they developed a new cycle which brought even more people and their money. We call this cycle tourism.

The influence and money affixed to tourism caused a tectonic shift in the way of life for this people until their culture wasn't so particular, their way of life not so unique. But at some point, the tourists themselves stopped caring so much, or maybe they never even noticed at all. The place and the history themselves had become symbols, abstractions which now held meaning and value in the far away places. And so the tourists kept rolling in.

At the end of this cycle lie the overcrowded roads and alleyways of touts, commercial businesses, and tour companies all selling, surviving off superficial reproductions of elements of that thing which once was. Along the way, the in-flux of tourists and money raised the base standard of living somewhat. However, this lift was likely not enjoyed equally across the community and perhaps created divides which did not exist before.

In the end the community gave up – not fully out of choice but not fully against their own will – an old way of life in exchange for dependency on a system of tourism which seeks to universalize the particular and doesn't give a damn about them in the end.

* * *

Now, take this story and multiply it by something called the internet and by an entire generation of bored, anxious, wealthy kids desperately seeking significance and authenticity in a world devoid of either. What you get is the above story reproducing on a massive scale the world over at a pace that would make your head spin.

Chapter 6

I can only answer the question 'What am I to do?' If I can first answer the prior question 'Of what story or stories do I find myself a part?'
Alasdair MacIntyre, After Virtue

In the same way I didn't want to "find myself a part" of *that* story for the people of Wadi Rum, I don't want to be part of *this* story for the people of Dana and their epically beautiful, still unscathed *Wadi*.

The bigger story, the cycle is out of my immediate control. Yet, as with all such systems, we each play a small role regardless of our relative awareness.

Travel – particularly international travel – is not a light treading activity. It is immensely costly – monetarily, environmentally, and otherwise.

As I travel more and more, I'm increasingly aware of and confused by the often harmful systems I both feed into and benefit from as a visitor from a rich country. I'm often struck by the disproportionate effect my actions are somehow able to have on the economies, ecologies, and human lives I encounter.

It is these human lives, the people we meet on the road, which are the hardest to remake in our own image. We may effortlessly, subconsciously reshape their lands with little more than Instagram posts and TripAdvisor reviews. However, a people are not conquered so easily, so silently as a place.

As our unwitting conquest to remake communities and individuals in our own western image falls short, we slowly begin to resent some differences between "theirs" and "ours" while embracing or glorifying others. Resentment gets us nowhere, of course. But neither does glorification of ancient communal narratives which we cannot authentically inherit and will never truly understand.

* * *

It was a long day in the bed of that truck back in Wadi Rum. In just over 7 hours, we stopped at nearly a dozen desert sights on the "circuit." We climbed up to Lawrence's Spring, where the famed "Brit of Arabia" first found water. We saw the petroglyphs, hiked through slot canyons, and stopped to gawk at rocks shaped like mushrooms, bridges, and elephants.

It was all spectacular. Honestly, it was too much to absorb in a single day, but I had to be back in Amman for work on Monday.

For the night, we stopped to rest at an "authentic Bedouin camp." There was a delicious local meal, an epic sunset, and a desert glamping campsite. At the end of the evening, we gathered around a fire to talk with our guides and members of the tribe.

"No, no one really lives in the desert anymore. We all moved to the village a few decades back," answers Marok, an older gentleman and leader of this tour company. "It is just easier now and that is where there's work."

"Don't you miss it?" asks an Australian girl from our group. "I mean, the way it was *before*?"

Marok pauses to think and says slowly, "Well, yes. There are elements. I appreciated having my children at home to help with the chores and tend the sheep. This is how my people always lived and yes, I miss it, but there is no going back now."

"But now your children can attend school, right?" she asks.

"Yes, in fact, we have no choice in the matter. School is mandatory and it draws them away from the village once they are grown."

"So, they are able to find new jobs and choose what kind of life they want? That's great!"

"Well, they can choose, but not to live the way we did before."

Silence.

This conversation is not unlike others I hear on the road. The traveler wants to remember how things were in yesteryear. We want a piece of the past. Yet in the end, we cannot bear it. The irreconcilable inconsistencies behind a romanticized past are too much for us. We seek only a stylized western conception of things which once were.

We long nostalgically for the picturesque particularities our culture has long since eschewed in the name of "progress" and "freedom." Yet, as we catch a glimpse, we are confronted again by our nagging insistence to read the universal into our specifically western late-modern cultural paradigms.

And this is not solely the domain of naive, adventure-seeking backpackers.

* * *

Of course, cross-cultural engagement is about more than imposing and coercing and shaping narratives. It is about learning and reflecting and considering what to apply and what to abandon in our communities back home.

For this reason, amongst others, travel is not an unmitigated evil. Despite what these initial chapters may seem to imply, condemnation of travel (or other wealthy western millennial pursuits) is not the moral of my story. I do think the particular combination of these "things that we do" can work together to contribute to systems well beyond our grasp, implicating us in realities we probably wouldn't like if we could only see them unfold.

Yet here we are at this unique moment in history where a lucky subset of people is able to move and live basically without restriction. Getting paid to do so with regularity is almost too much to fully grasp.

In a sense, this is great. Travel offers unprecedented opportunities to expand the mind. It relieves us from the ignorance of the particular and the parochial even as it fails to provide a universal answer to that particularity. It endows us with a love and an awe for place, for culture, for experience outside of (and often contradictory to) our own.

Through exposure to places, cultures, and experiences slightly less whitewashed than our own, we might just stumble a step or two closer toward real fulfillment and significance and maybe even toward that elusive thing we call truth.

This, though, is the hard part of travel, the seeing of things through a different lens, the learning to live honestly with new knowledge of differing perspectives, beliefs, experiences. For, even in the midst of the very act which makes this enlightenment possible, we fight against its potential good.

Faced with the discomfort of difference – of cultures incompatible with our own – we all too often use our resources to pad our travel experiences, and, back home, our very lives from such painful uncertainty.

Travel, if there is a chance for it be anything more than a wasteful exercise in self-indulgence, must resist, must consciously effort *not* to find ease. Rather, it should embolden us to wrestle with the tension and the discomfort and the uncertainty we see to the point where we begin to glimpse that beautiful horizon of recognition, respect, and empathy of people, culture, and place not our own.

If we are open and lucky enough, some moments of this journey might just test this posture of empathy more than others, bending and re-shaping our worldviews and identities, shaking our conceptions of who we are and what we do to the very core.

Chapter 7

If we cannot tell a story about what happened to us, nothing has happened to us.
James P. Carse, Finite and Infinite Games

In some ways, not much "has happened." Not much changed during the three decades filling the pages between my first Texan truck bed ride, my 2019 jaunt through Wadi Rum, and my decidedly unfree writing desk today, here, amidst the pandemic and government-lockdown decimated metropolis of Phnom Penh, Cambodia.

I'm still the four-year-old kid breathing deeply into the dry, rushing West Texas wind, inspired and blinded by the limitless possibilities of my own perceived potential.

I'm still hoping to build a superficial identity for myself through my travels, my possessions, my career, my hobbies; to share this "self" with the world and through that act of sharing to fill something missing inside me.

I'm still exploring and conquering and imposing my views, preferences, and tastes on people who never asked for my opinion.

I'm still, often, living my life with a brazen, willing blindness to the consequences of my choices or the endless complexity of the world as it is.

In truth, all that has happened, all that has changed is the emergence of a series of stories. These stories were forged in those sacred, profane moments where we encounter the individuals and communities who welcome us into their own stories along the winding road of life. These stories now form a broader narrative arc which whispers meaning into my lost wanderings.

In a very real sense, stories are all we have to guide us toward the illusive concept of truth in this finite, fleeting life. So, from another point of view, given the stories I now tell, everything has changed.

* * *

I write today as a member of a peculiar community which bases our lives and wanderings and understanding of truth on another set of stories – stories of a man who died and defeated death over 2,000 years ago. I believe in the power of these stories, told in love and in the guiding light of a historical community of stumbling believers, to push us toward glimpses of truth amidst a world of lies.

In these pages, I add my own stories of misguided seeking and searching to the blundering, imperfect, lost, and wandering history we call the Christian Church. This starting point may make some of what I say incomprehensible to those who live outside this community. Or, perhaps, it might begin to raise questions about the substitutes we all seek in our grasping, wander-lost search for meaning and significance and joy.

If my coming of-age-journey is to offer something of broader worth, it is a hopeful plea – to myself and those around me – to stop this grasping once and for all. It is a humble challenge for us each to open our hands and release our illusion of control in surrender to the deeper realities of this fleeting life.

This is a story of how my own stumbling journey through childhood, college, and beyond awakened me to the freedom which can emerge from such a posture of surrender.

Section 2

On young Achilles

Chapter 8

I am very special.
There is no one quite like me.
I'm one of a kind.
As you can plainly see.
When I grow old
I don't know what I will be.
But I know it will be great
Because, I will be me.
Anonymous

There I am. It's the first day of first grade. We've already gone over the fact that I'm a precocious white boy from a stable, loving, upper middle class family. So, essentially, I have all the material advantages and crutches the world can offer.

And this poem is how they start the class.

Each morning, we recite our pledge of allegiance to our own unique wonderfulness. Fittingly, the ritual poem occurs directly after we declare our loyalty to the human contrived nation-state into which we were all unwittingly born.

Each morning, we repeat these liturgies and forget in unison the simple fact that we did not choose to be born in this country or to this century which so values our collective individuality.

Each morning, we recognize in our words, if not our minds, that we live in a very special place and time where public education is mostly free and generally good and quite effective at indoctrinating us with the values held most dear by our society.

Each morning, we gently mix with our words the key pillars of our culture – the progressive temple of individual preeminence and the conservative altar of (sometimes) subtle nationalism.

* * *

This scene is not unique to my story. Rather, it plays out daily in classrooms and minds across our nation. And that seemingly heroic call for absolute individualistic liberty, personal expression, and economic opportunity turns sinister when aimed at groups which seek different, more particular ends.

Nowhere within our borders is this fact more clear than in the accommodation of the Christian Church. This community was formed two millennia ago as the radical incarnation of a crucified Christ – a people embracing as birthrights their own physical oppression, marginalization, and martyrdom. I'm not talking about the sort of twisted "martyr syndrome" frequently displayed by American Christians afraid of losing political or cultural influence. I'm talking about getting literally killed for your form of life.

Reconciling a mandate to usher in your own physical suffering and even death with the American Dream is utterly impossible. The evangelical "church" as it exists today in this country is a validation of that impossibility. It is lightyears away from its historical center. Rather, it finds itself fully remade into a quintessentially American institution, worshipping individualism, nationalism, and self-preservation as its highest dogmas.

But it is not just the American Church which finds itself adrift from its authentic, historical identity in our present society.

Small communities are written off as nosy and insular and economically non-viable. Gradually, they lose themselves to decay and depression and population flight.

Across the westernized world, minority languages are snubbed as stifling as they are increasingly replaced with the lingua franca of efficiency.

Traditional values are increasingly condemned as imposing. Acceptable, neutered versions of those values are unable to mold particular communities in any direction other than the late-modern American one.

Here, in the US and throughout our global hegemony, we've bowled over these and other "obstacles" to progress or brought them into the fold. So universal, so natural is this scene for us, that we forget how very odd it is from a global perspective, not to mention from a historical one.

Elsewhere, this cultural takeover is less uniform, the uprooting and remaking less complete.

According to historian Meic Pearse, author of *Why the Rest Hates the West*, this forgetting, this willing ignorance of our cultural blind spots leaves us tragically unaware of how we are viewed beyond our borders – as "dangerously seductive, but domineering barbarians." Across most of the rest of the world, the liberal-democratic values we are indoctrinating our children to internalize and promote are viewed very differently.

As I sat in that first grade classroom basking in my own uniqueness, ecstatic at the vague inevitability of my own immortality, confident in the universality of my immature western faith and worldview, a rage was simmering on the other side of the globe.

* * *

Fast forward a few years. It's seventh grade now. Our class project this week is to draw a picture of ourselves as grown-ups, say 10 years into our career.

We have a week where we learn about and talk about all kinds of careers. Everyone is discussing what they want to be and imaginations are going wild.

At the end of the week all the pictures are up on the wall, and everyone is looking at the drawings. We're trying to guess who drew which ones and the different careers the drawings depict.

In our class of 25, there are at least three doctors, two

firefighters, several soldiers, a "computer guy" or two, a handful of teachers, three businesswomen, a lawyer, several artists, and at least five professional athletes.

There is also a blond guy with jeans, a T-shirt, a leather jacket, and aviator glasses.

He was supposed to be cool and confident and mysterious and interesting. To be sure, among the myriad drawings, he emanated those traits best. The problem was that he didn't know exactly what he was supposed to be.

He definitely did not want one of those "normal" career tracks, and it had to be different from what the other kids said. He just didn't know what.

When my turn came, I was still fumbling with what to say. Up to that point in my life, my days were pretty much laser-focused on playing street football. When no game was possible, I was also passionate about setting off firecrackers, solving imaginary mysteries with my little sister in our backyard, riding my bike as fast as possible down steep hills, climbing to the tops of trees, and showering as infrequently as possible.

Of course, I couldn't say "professional football player." Such was my actual dream at that moment, but it felt far too dangerous to put it out there and set an actual, externally known goal.

For some reason, I had in my head to say fighter pilot, I think. To be honest, this would've been as good a guess as any at that point since the NFL was probably never in the cards.

But then, the girl right in front of me said she wanted to be a pilot and I had to change tack. Going with pilot directly after pilot was entirely off the table. Plus, there was the question of *cooties* if I said the same thing as the cute girl before me.

It is embarrassing, but I think I blurted out "Film Director" or something. Embarrassing, not because film directors are inherently lame, but because, at the time, I thought it sounded kind of edgy and cool. In reality, the idea of going into the film industry (particularly behind camera) has never crossed my mind or sounded the remotest bit appealing. But that is what came out.

Even at this young age, I was totally lost in my confused quest for uniqueness and competency. I didn't know who I was or what I wanted to be and I was too embarrassed to say something which might be close to the truth.

* * *

The very next week, we started Homer's *The Iliad*. A dialogue in the opening act struck a chord with me as I wrestled with my failure to choose a direction for my life. Achilles offers a chilling account of his hubris and lostness and dreams of immortality; qualities, even at that young age, I recognized in myself.

In this conversation, Achilles' mother pleads with him to stay, encouraging him with all he has to live for:

"If you stay here with me, with your family, you shall enjoy a long and peaceful life. You shall have children and they will have children. They shall love you and when you are gone they will remember you."

"Hmm," I think to myself. "They will remember you. That's really nice. Sounds promising."

But then she goes and ruins her case in the very next line.

"But when your children are dead, and their children after them, your name will be lost."

Sitting in my bed, reading this line over and over, I craved, yearned for something more. How "special," how "no one quite like me" could I really be if the best I could hope for was a normal life in a good community with a loving family?

At the pinnacle of all of human history, as a winner of the proverbial global, historic gene lottery, how could my fate be so humble, so ordinary as this?

Even today, with all the awareness and know-how, I am

vulnerable to this trap. I am drawn insatiably by a desire to impact the world far beyond the confines of a single life.

Yet, I'm given a certain amount of time on this earth. It *should* be enough to love and remember the important people in my life – hopefully to be loved and remembered by them someday. My motivation for action *should* be simply to love people when and where and how I have the opportunity.

But, the safety, the security, and the normalcy of this life – confined to the 80 something years, if I'm lucky – is somehow not enough for my pride and selfishness and disordered longing for infinite freedom.

In my more inspired (or narcissistic) moments, I tell myself this desire doesn't have to be all bad. I want to be remembered for good, *right*? I want to be remembered as someone who "served God," *right*? I want to be remembered as someone who made a difference, someone who changed the world positively, *right*?

Above all that though, I know my true desire – like Achilles – is just that. *I want to be remembered.*

"If you go to Troy, no one shall earn more glory than you. Men will tell stories of your victories for thousands of years. The world will remember your name."

My heart rings out more than I'd like to admit when I read those words. When I read them for the first time, back on my bed in seventh grade, I knew instantly what he would decide, what I would decide.

Chapter 9

What happens when a 'gifted child' finds himself in a wilderness where he's stripped of any way of proving his worth? What does he do when there's nothing he can do, when there's no audience to applaud his performance, when he faces a cold, silent indifference if not hostility? His world falls to pieces. The soul hungry for approval starves in the desert like that. It reduces the compulsive achiever to something little, utterly ordinary. Only then is he able to be loved or truly love himself.
Belden Lane, Backpacking with the Saints

I grew up in a football family and Cowboys were king. Some of my earliest, fondest memories were on the couch with my mom and grandpa, rooting for our team.

Until Jerry Jones displaced Tom Landry that is. Then, my mom swore them off until the day he dies.

I'm not joking. She still roots actively with me, but now it is for whoever the Cowboys play each week, and she has a shirt where she writes all their home losses in permanent marker.

In spite of my mom's (clearly serious) issues, I grew up a Cowboys fan. Though there were probably many before it, the first game I vividly remember watching was Super Bowl XXX when quarterback Troy Aikman or "Eightman" (at the time, I believed he was #8 to correspond with his mispronounced name) led an effective dismantling of the hated Pittsburgh Steelers.

As I watched Mr. "Eightman" and his Cowboys soar to victory on the world's largest stage, I knew instantly where I would find my immortality.

What I did not realize at the time was that our family was not blessed greatly in terms of size or brute strength. Not a single person in my immediate family line is over 5'10" or 170lb.

Nonetheless, I could see a quintessentially American mirage

of immortality in such a future, and I wanted it. For endless hours, I played catch in the yard with my dad, pickup football in the street with my friends, and pretend Super Bowl in our basement – diving repeatedly to catch passes from a "bounce back" toy onto some worn out mattresses.

When I reached middle school, I rallied the troops at recess each day to play football, and that is absolutely all I ever wanted to do. I didn't have much of an arm so the "Eightman" dream quickly faded. But I could get open, I could catch anything my hands touched, and I'd be damned if I wasn't willing to sacrifice my body for the glory of even the most meaningless catch in the lowest stakes game. Thus, I became a wide receiver and cornerback.

My true athletic advantage was lurking in the background. I couldn't see it at the time, though everyone around me did and was greatly annoyed by it. This advantage was the simple fact that I could, strangely, almost mythically, keep playing at full, break-neck intensity for hours after everyone else had to call it quits.

I thought I just loved football more than everyone else. In reality, I had a physical gift and was gradually, unconsciously honing it with each passing game.

The spring of my eighth-grade year (if not before), I should have recognized this gift and its implications, but my eyes were still set on Super Bowl glory.

That year, my school hosted a jog-a-thon fundraiser. I was mowing a bunch of lawns and figured I'd ask my clients for sponsorship. Turns out none of them thought I'd make it very far, so they all pledged by the lap.

The morning of the event, I ate a big breakfast and was brimming with energy. The air was cool. The gun went off and I started running, just trying – like all the other kids with no knowledge of pacing strategy – to keep up with the front of the pack.

After a lap or two, everyone else had fallen back, but I felt good so I just kept going.

I got into this little game where I wanted to see how many times I could lap a certain person or how long I could keep a certain level of intensity.

The minutes and the laps flew by.

At around 45 minutes, something strange, something that had never really happened before, suddenly clicked inside me, and I couldn't let myself slow down.

For some reason, I got in my head that I needed to finish 40 laps, an even 10 miles. Between now panting breaths, I figured out the pace I needed to get there. Everything in my body said quit. There was no real reason to continue. I had never pushed this hard or been in so much pain in my entire life, but I couldn't stop, couldn't let up. I just kept finding these new planes of energy hidden inside.

As time expired, I heaved my body across the finish line for lap number 40, took another few steps, and subsequently vomited all over the place.

My pace worked out to an even 6:00/mile, 10 miles in exactly 60 minutes as a 12-year-old. This time positioned me to enter ninth grade as one of the fastest runners on my high-school cross country team and put me in range for a D1 Cross-Country Scholarship, again, as a 12-year-old.

My "talent," as it were, was a high threshold for cardiovascular endurance.

Years later, a collegiate track coach would shake his head at this story and tell me someone should have put me immediately into a Junior Olympic training program.

But it wasn't that people didn't tell me it was great. It wasn't that I didn't get any good guidance or encouragement.

It was simply that I didn't see running long distances at relatively high speeds as a path which could ever lead to glory and the ever-present illusion of immortality.

So, 3 months later, as a 4'11" 95lb freshman I signed up for the football team at the country's largest high school.

That high school was one of the state's perennial football powerhouses. My senior year, 14 of our starting 22 got big D1 scholarships. And they all weighed more as freshmen than I will ever weigh. They all bench-pressed more and ran faster 40-yard dashes and hit harder and had more facial hair as freshmen than I ever will.

Needless to say, I got the crap kicked out of me and warmed the bench the entire season.

Nonetheless, wearing the jersey to class on game day made me feel important and special. My high school was a big place, and I was on the football team.

Running cross country never entered my mind.

* * *

I lifted weights the entire off season and worked all the way up to 102lbs. I wanted to make this work and I knew it was just a matter of time before I got my chance. But then I broke my arm two months before the start of the season. Football was graciously over for me.

A dream died in that hospital room and with it, my primary motivation and wellspring of ambition.

Instead of drifting aimlessly, my parents insisted that I do something, anything, with my time after school. Sensibly, they nudged me gently toward cross country.

The first practice, I ran a 6-ish mile tempo with the fastest seniors. I hadn't run more than 40 yards at a time since that eighth grade jog-a-thon, 18 months prior. But I still pretty much rolled with them.

I felt some discomfort during the run and somewhat ill afterward. Also, I wasn't decidedly the very fastest person on the team from Day 1. With these data points in-hand, I immediately decided trying at this sport just wasn't going to do it for me.

For the rest of the season and for the next three years, I was technically part of the cross country and track teams. But I didn't ever do more than a light jog in practice, and I rarely participated in meets.

I'd find ways to sneak off just as the team headed out for a long run and then slink back in at the end as if I were just slow.

I'd take up pole vaulting as a way to maximize my time sitting around and to limit the number of tough workouts I had to endure.

I'd make excuses to my parents about why I couldn't go to meets or why I needed to miss practices altogether on certain days.

In general, I made certain never to apply myself, never to allow myself to experience pain, never to push myself anywhere close to my limits or even to the point where I'd have to admit I was trying.

At the time, I didn't know why I was doing this to myself. It certainly didn't make me feel good to slack off and be viewed as a scrub.

Deep down, I was mourning. I was mourning the loss of a false identity which I'd held tightly for close to a decade.

In my mind, in my heart, in those critical moments where one either finds their calling or misses it, I knew beyond a shadow of a doubt that I was born to be a professional football player.

* * *

In college, I somehow re-discovered the joy of running, first as a pastime and later as a walk-on athlete. I reconnected with the freedom, the pain, the unadulterated joy which comes from a body and soul doing precisely what they were made to do — flying free, uninhibited, racing with the wind.

For over a decade now, I've re-engaged tenderly and at times passionately with the sport, with the life I forsook as a 12-year-old when I substituted reality for a stylized version of it.

I've run hard these last years, pushed and shaped my body with the discipline of a runner and the knowledge I was once born to do so.

Today, I'm fast for an amateur runner. I sometimes place in my age group and occasionally win local races. I enjoy setting and meeting personal, incremental goals for improvement.

But I missed my chance for glory. In all my training runs, road races, crazy trail runs, and PRs, I've never once flirted with the upper limits of potential that a lifetime of disciplined training might have honed.

I will never be the runner I could've become when I was a professional football player at age 12.

Too often, I find myself in similar traps. I look ahead to how my future situation might transcend the monotony of my particular place on this earth. In so doing, I risk missing the race before me. And there are races more important than those run with feet and lungs.

Chapter 10

To imagine a world in which war has been abolished requires that we live in a community that celebrates and shares a language that helps us see such an alternative world.
John Howard Yoder

They say you remember where you were when it happened. I was in school, 6.5 miles from the Pentagon. We were just entering second period when they made the announcement. Our parents would be there soon to pick us up.

I went out to my locker and grabbed my dirty football cleats. I decided to leave behind a half finished drawing of my "cool guy" fictitious adult self.

My dad worked in Crystal City, directly across the street from the Pentagon, but had telecommuted that day.

Within two hours, our family was all at home, huddled around the TV, praying for our country and our leaders and the families who would never be all together again.

Just a few days later, mourning and meditation turned to action. On the national scale, a cohesive narrative was solidifying. This was us against them. Our nation under God indivisibly against people who hate Christianity, Democracy, and Apple Pie. Axes of evil formed, lines were drawn, and everyone was suddenly either for or against us.

I vividly remember this new, starkly black and white caricature being painted over a once multi-colored world map. As an American kid, it was comforting and focusing to feel this strong message, reducing an infinitely complex world into two oversimplified choices, America vs. Evil.

As a nation, 9/11 was, perhaps, our last "holy war" moment. That day in September – whether spent huddled around our TVs or fighting through smoke and soot or waiting to hear from loved ones who would never call – was a final rallying cry uniting the world's greatest nation and its security-grasping people under the banner of a common cause.

And unite us it did. 10 days later, I remember my own family huddling around the TV again with the rest of the nation as we learned more of the "plan."

According to Gallup, 92% of the country approved of our president after his post-9/11 State of the Union address. Ninety-two percent agreed with this "us against them" mentality, this need to come together and punch back hard. Never before in polling history had so many people been so quantifiably united behind an elected leader. And since democracy was now somehow interchangeable as Christian doctrine, the polls signaled to us that God himself was on board.

Yet, there was little of the divine in this policy. There was never a mention of what might be broken about ourselves or our relationship with state power which led us to this point where peace was an impossibility. Few thoughts were directed toward envisioning how we might change our posture toward the world to prevent such violence in the future.

At the core of President Bush's base were Christian folks like me. Christians who had become accustomed to being protected physically and ideologically by the red, white, and blue. Christians who were comfortable propping up their "freedom" with relative wealth and violence-buffered security. Christians blind to the reality of what such "blessings" implied for the rest of the world. Christians who fundamentally accepted state-led violence against those who persecute Christians and Americans globally.

It wasn't on 9/11 that these beliefs formed. I had heard them implied in church and para-church settings my whole life. Yet, in this moment of great crisis for our country, the church expressed an utter lack of coherence with its own narrative. We revealed clearly how, for far too long, we had been cheaply substituting our spiritual call to be set apart for something far more earthly.

We found ourselves deeply, utterly enmeshed, comfortably blinded by our position near the helm of great human power. Alongside our countrymen, we were quick to anger, to scapegoat, to be indiscriminately violent, to find fault external, conscious only to imagined purity within.

To be clear, this is a totally reasonable reaction for a human nation-state. Indeed, for a country such as ours to remain intact at such a pivotal moment in our history, it was the only option.

The Church, though, is not faced with such all or nothing choices. We are not born to be creatures of war. If we truly claim to follow a crucified Christ, we must remember Jesus' own radical response to violence. We, like Him, are called to release our illusions of control over our own physical safety. We are called to be different even – or perhaps especially – if that difference means our material security is threatened.

We were not different though. I was not different.

Almost in unison, we revealed ourselves as Americans first and told the world Christ was synonymous with, or subsidiary to our great nation. And the global church suffered immensely from this untruthful account of our deepest allegiance.

Today, the world turns as "normal" once more. Unifying wounds of the past are no longer strong enough to hold the bond.

We are brow-beaten daily with disturbing images, trends, and figures to the point of immunity – or at least paralyzing shock. The post-9/11 unity America once stood upon was demonstrated as false and short-lived. Today, our "normalcy" is increasingly distracted, polarized, calloused, uncertain.

The "United" States of America no longer huddles together in spirit, but in myriad competing factions, each numb to the reality of violence and chaos in our world, each seeking its own preservation.

Due to our exceptional ability to inflict violence on a grand scale, America remains intact physically. However, its soul now lies in splinters, as does, in many ways, the world it created.

In today's fragmented, unsafe, forgetful world, we, as Christians, gain something immeasurable. This past world where Christianity brought with it power and influence now crumbles around us. Though the remnants of that power still stand for now, we find ourselves in the process of becoming free to be our own people, as opposed to being people of a human nation – even a great one.

We must recognize this moment, this opportunity to shake free the centuries' long watering down, humanizing, accommodating of our tradition.

But, let me not hide behind the collective "we."

I did this to myself after all. I grew comfortable with my "privilege" – those trappings of worldly power and security which I did not earn but which deeply distort my view of the world and my place in it. In the arms of this privilege, my childhood was richly "blessed" in terms of opportunities to construct superficial, heroic, often deluded identities for myself. And I – when these trappings were threatened – saw the violence and injustice of war as the only option to sustain this unpromised, unfulfilling way of life.

As a teenager, I was developing quickly in the direction of the great liturgies and mythologies of our culture. This was tragically in unison with my fallen, broken church, the most American of institutions intended originally as something far different.

And this process of formation had only just begun.

Chapter 11

To be human is to be on the move, pursuing something, after something. We are like existential sharks: we have to move to live.
James K.A. Smith, You Are What You Love

I never did quite get my wires straight enough to effectively pursue athletics anywhere near my potential. But playing in the Super Bowl wasn't my only dream in those days.

Perhaps it was the early feeling of "freedom" I felt in the back of a truck in my father's arms.

Perhaps it was the aftermath of my encounter with the Greek bard or my unconscious longing to forge images of a life immortal using the cultural symbols of our time.

Perhaps it's just the fact that my heart pumps the blood of a displaced redneck kid molded first and deepest by the warm winds and rich soil of the great state of Texas.

Regardless of the reason, it was somewhere around my thirteenth birthday when my first conscious capitalist yearnings took root. I felt, for the first time, that now familiar void of something missing in my life. I desperately needed to own this one material thing and – in some ethereal way – to be defined, set free by that act of conquest and possession.

The vision was clear. As the prospect of high school and adolescence loomed, I needed a shiny red truck.

There were just two problems.

First, there was the aching slowness of time as it presents itself to an impetuous adolescent. I was thirteen. You can't go flying down so much as a back country road in northern Virginia until you are 15.5. You can't do so *sans père* for another nine months after that. So, I had a bit of a wait ahead of me.

The second problem was cash flow. As I would soon discover, my parents were not your typical northern VA enablers. While they probably could've afforded to promise me a jalopy for my sweet 16, such a classic parenting mistake was not in the cards.

"Great!" my dad said enthusiastically. "Sounds like you need to get a job."

After a look through the car ads in the local paper (yes, internet was still in its infancy back in 2001) and some quick calculations, I realized my allowance just wasn't going to cut it.

$2.50 per week multiplied by three years, factoring in inflation and the odd ice cream cone here and there, was still going to leave me, oh, $8,000 or so short on my dream car, a bright red 2000 Dodge Dakota.

The next day, I came back and asked my dad for employment. He looked through his job board and came back with an offer I couldn't refuse. $5 a week to mow, edge, and clean the yard. It wasn't good pay, but for an hour's worth of work, it tripled my weekly take. After a failed first attempt at high stakes negotiation, I accepted.

Expenses were fairly limited at this point. Aside from the occasional fines imposed by my mother for assorted acts of mischief, they were, in fact, zero.

That summer, I didn't spend a dime. I added to my piggy bank $7.50 a week and couldn't believe my luck. The next summer and the one after that and each one for the rest of my childhood, I'd mow that yard, and then my neighbors' yards, and then their neighbors' yards as my piggy bank and conception of the value of money began to mature.

Those early years on the market economy proved fruitful. I grew my first business; picked up off-season shifts at the local deli; and, eventually, saved enough to purchase my truck – a gorgeous bright red 2000 Dodge Dakota I was sure would complete my self-ascribed identity.

* * *

Eighteen years on, after returning from that thought-provoking trip to Jordan, I found myself in uncharted territory. For the first time in over a decade, I did not have an international trip planned and did not know when my next might be.

My body cried out for relief after the inconsistent sleep and tense muscles which come from months and years of nights on the road and endless hours in jostling planes, buses, truck beds and the like.

But my need for rest quickly paled in comparison to the rising of a somewhat unaware, undefined yet deeply familiar and all-encompassing general sense of anxiety.

It made no difference that I loved my home and wanted to spend time investing in my community with my lovely wife.

It made no difference that I now found myself disillusioned in many ways with a life devoted to seeking and striving after personal transcendence and experiential acquisition out on the open road.

This was all I knew. I had no experience facing the pressures of adult life without the ability to escape. Travel had always been that escape.

It was also more than escape which I sought and, on some level, found in travel. It was identity. Travel was something unique about me, something from a certain perspective I was comparatively "good" at, if "good" is indeed something we can still define.

With this broken excuse for identity temporarily removed, I had to find something else. If I couldn't travel and explore, then, perhaps, I might return to conquest via consumption.

* * *

In 1994, a Japanese automaker took a risk with a totally new vehicle concept which was introduced as XA10 Chassis 4-wheel drive Recreational Activity Vehicle. The concept featured – for the first time all together – "a unibody chassis, fully independent suspension, 4-wheel drive, high ground clearance and car, not truck, in mentality, construction, and parts" (Jalopnik, 2015).

Two years later, they took an even bigger risk and put this radical idea into production under a new, more market-friendly name: Rav4.

With the Rav4, Toyota sought to diverge for the first time from the "traditional model of slapping a station wagon body on a truck chassis and calling it an SUV." Toyota realized, before anyone else, that young, adventurous, pioneering Americans wanted some utility and some adventure, but they also wanted something fun.

Years before I could even drive, Toyota understood me. It just took me another 25 years to catch onto the vision.

Today, the RAV4 is just another bloated, boring, commodity in the crowded crossover market, but it wasn't always this way. In 1996 and 1997, Toyota produced about 1,000 two-door RAVs with removable doors and roof panels which look like mini Safari vehicles.

I had to have one.

Whenever they came for sale, these 2-door Ravs were within my price range... when they came for sale. For two months, I scoured the internet for one, but no one was selling.

It was certifiably time for our family to get a second car. Our jobs were now on opposite sides of town and the lofty idea of bike-as-transportation quickly lost its appeal in practice.

Each day I didn't buy a car was a major inconvenience as I needed to bike everywhere. But such sacrifices are trivial when faced with an opportunity to acquire something you feel completes your superficial identity, right?

The irony of this obsession – in the midst of a longer reflection on how material substitutes had too deeply shaped, even defined my identity – did not escape me. Yet, as with travel, excitement for a cool car didn't strike me as wrong in and of itself, so the search continued.

Eventually, I found it: a Silver 1996 2-door hardtop from the original owner. It was a good price. The owner was willing to let me have a mechanic look it over. It had (relatively) low miles and was in good shape for its age. Just one problem.

It was over 2,000 miles away.

One-way flights to Denver were cheap and I am richly blessed with a lover-comrade incredibly tolerant and understanding of my impetuous nature.

The next day, I was on a plane.

Driving "Burt" back across the country, I was struck by two undeniable facts.

On one hand, I do indeed love this car. It's no truck bed, but with the doors and roof off, the wind whips my hair and courses over my face in a way which has always awakened me. Driving stick makes me feel deeply connected to the road. Driving something with a history makes me feel somehow united with the past. Driving with a bag of essential tools and never knowing when I might break down and need to solve a mechanical problem lends a sense of adventure and risk and ingenuity to the otherwise dull task of a daily commute or cross-country drive.

On the other hand, every time I look at this car, I know and see again, for the millionth time how insatiably, undeniably I am drawn to material substitutes for identity and purpose.

Whether I am traveling to an exotic locale or acquiring a fun, attention-grabbing yet decrepit vehicle, I signal that I am looking for something.

I recognize now – yet still somehow lack the character to correct – a desperate seeking for something I will never find in such pursuits. And after all these years, I am still seeking with an intensity and frequency only possible for someone who already has too much.

Chapter 12

We seek the infinite worth of that which is seemingly worthless and the infinite worthlessness of that which is seemingly so valued.
Dietrich Bonhoeffer, Ethics

"Don't forget. Everyone is replaceable."

I was seventeen the first time I heard those words. My teenage ego had swollen predictably as the weekend shift (scrubbing grease off floor-mats at the local deli) transitioned into something a bit more dignified.

Promotions were rolling in at regular intervals – from grease-scraper to dish-washer, from dish-washer to cashier, from cashier to line cook, from line cook to shift manager. At $9.25, my hourly wages had surged at a rate of 38 percent a year over my first eighteen months of employment. My hours, too, reflected a rapidly rising status – from a once-a-week charity shift offered to the child of loyal customers to a dependable part-time worker's thirty hours per week, just beneath the benefits threshold.

"Don't forget. Everyone is replaceable."

This phrase about our imminent replaceability was repeated by my father in various conversations throughout the early years of my engagement with the market economy. It wasn't a mean-spirited remark. Rather, it was a mantra that had clearly served as a stabilizing reminder over the course of his own often unpredictable career. I heard it about me, about himself, and about others who might somehow have forgotten the contingent nature of their employment.

I would soon learn that one could be replaced for myriad reasons. Technology could render a role redundant. Political winds could leave a position out in the cold during a restructure. Budget cuts could reduce the number of available jobs, generating a zero-sum competition to demonstrate value.

And there, perhaps, was the core of the message: value. The unspoken instruction for successfully navigating the disorienting world of market-based human interchangeability was to identify opportunities for maximizing one's value to the system.

At the deli, I realized, I added value in three primary ways.

First, I demonstrated the efficiency of my labor. I used my youthful energy to finish dishes better and faster, to carry more bags of trash, to assemble a platter of panini with greater aplomb. In future jobs, I would summon a maniacal will for generating efficiencies and economies of scale, which allowed me to achieve greater volumes of productivity than my peers as an individual contributor, and eventually a team leader. Perhaps more importantly, efficiency increased my value as an employee in direct proportion to how it reduced the value of other employees: often these nameless others could be replaced by my streamlined processes or superior techniques.

Second, I demonstrated the dependability of my labor. I showed up early and stayed late. I could do this because I didn't have kids at home, a second job, errands to run, or other responsibilities. I chose to continue this habit throughout the early stages of my career because I found working longer engendered the admiration of supervisors, who tend to notice such things. Doing so also offered me a chance to "get ahead" while others rested.

Third, I demonstrated the versatility of my labor. I again leveraged the privilege of my youth, my lack of other responsibilities, and my (comparatively speaking) elite education to learn new skills. With them, I sought further opportunities for innovation, process improvement, and the like. I found ways to put these innovations to use for the benefit of my employers and my personal brand therein.

Through these various "value-adding" strategies, I attained

success of a sort. If nothing else, I found ways to be viewed at the deli and beyond as valuable enough to keep around and occasionally to be promoted over "less valuable" colleagues.

In practice, value creation is always comparative. In a world of expanding commodification and shrinking margins across all sectors, only those deemed to add the most value will thrive. It's a system that privileges the already privileged and reinforces the pathological society-wide narrative of human interchangeability.

Once we believe the primary thrust of our jobs is a zero-sum competition, we buy into an exploitative system and disregard the more authentic reality in which we are all equal before our Maker. In so doing, we forget that others are more than their relative place in the pecking order. We forget that this pecking order, which now extends globally, is profoundly inhumane and unchristian in both its ideology and impact.

* * *

Fifteen years after leaving that deli, I observe daily some of the most grievous costs of the global economic system. Today, I work for an organization which partners with governments in an effort to end violent oppression against the world's poor. Amidst such work, I am confronted daily with the specific, brutal means by which our global economic system "creates value" for wealthy westerners, its undeniable winners.

Some forty million people today languish in a form of oppression we call *modern slavery*. Some are victims of class or gender-based exploitation, extortion, or coercion. The majority find themselves overpowered by the weight of that ultimate bourgeois technique for value creation – debt.

Debt has always served as a fixture of the global economy. Indeed, it is only through access to debt that we are able to so deliriously "add value" for ourselves – climbing the endless mountains of capital development, personal enrichment, and wealth-buffered security. But we see debt only as the winners of an unjust global contest. Those on the other side tell a very different story.

In Phnom Penh, Cambodia, from where I pen these words, I recently encountered the story of a young man named Ron. Ron used a microloan to purchase a plot of land for rubber production. When drought destroyed his crop, he was left with no viable alternative for employment and an unpayable debt to a local bank. And Ron is not alone. Cambodians today are drowning under the world's highest per capita microfinance burden.

In his desperation, Ron was lured across the border into Thailand by the promise of decent work. Instead, he found himself trapped on a boat. His passport was taken from him. He was forced to work long hours under brutal conditions with no pay for months on end. Ron found himself enslaved by a combination of debt and unchecked oppressive actors.

It wasn't just the traffickers and the abusive ship captain who made this possible. A long supply chain of more powerful actors "created value" via efficiencies and budget cuts and downward pressures that gradually provoked the inevitable conclusion. In the end, it proved more efficient to trade in slave labor than to recruit and pay fishermen fairly.

The value of Ron's life there at the bottom of the global fishing industry became precisely quantified by the insurmountable weight of his debt. This minuscule "value" was totally and completely divorced from his value as a human in the sight of God.

And the ultimate beneficiaries of this systematic global dehumanization? Western consumers demanding cheap and varied seafood.

The same story repeats itself across the Global South amongst those producing goods for the Global North in industries as varied as seafood, textile, electronic, agriculture, and construction, to name a few.

As a generation, we prioritize, compel, even moralize personal "value" acquisition – these misguided concepts of identity-via-possession and identity-via-experience – more than at any point in history. The result of this trend is a cultural and economic tidal wave, a disruptive and coercive cascade beyond the scope of our visibility or immediate empathy.

In the process, we crush the Rons of the world — the billions of not so privileged others making this whole lost and wandering thing possible.

* * *

My own journey toward broader realizations about the problematic nature of the world has been long, imperfect (often hypocritical) and totally non-linear.

In high school, my first truck helped form my deluded, selfish conception of human value and purpose. It also gave me an authentic experience with choice and consequence – after I crashed it and learned about the joys of insurance deductibles.

Real freedom is like a truck in that way, I guess.

Unfettered pursuit of freedom, that longing of being on our own with our choices and delusions of grandeur out on the open road, will leave us lost and wandering and alone. Shaped rightly, however, that disordered yearning can also bring out creativity, sacrifice, and purpose from even the most lost, lonely, and directionless wanderers among us.

It is not the freedom itself, not the material acquisition, not the limitless choice which forms us in this healthier manner. Rather, it is how we have been formed to utilize that freedom, those possessions, those choices.

In the end, regardless of how much freedom we might have (or not), it is virtue which gives us the ability to choose well. It is virtue which shapes us into responsible, productive members of a community. And virtue isn't something we're born with.

In this case, it was my parents' virtue more than my own – in giving me the choice and safe space to earn for myself what I thought I wanted and to teach me the value of responsibility and consequences when I had to pay for the wreck.

I think that's always how it is. We cannot become virtuous; we cannot even see what virtuous means without being formed by a community which embodies those virtues. The more deeply we are formed by a certain community, the freer we become to be ourselves within those particular confines.

In his Christian ethical classic *The Peaceable Kingdom*, theologian Stanley Hauerwas speaks beautifully of this gift within the community we call Church.

"That's why Christians need the Church," says Hauerwas. "I don't have any faith in myself of living a virtuous life; but if I am surrounded by other people who are also formed by the same commitments, then we've got a better chance. We need one another to live up to the wonderful invitation we've been given to be other than we are."

Learning to become "other than we are" is an absolute must for a redneck kid from Texas, a hyper-individualized millennial living in a uniquely American bubble. It is a must for a delusional 95-lb professional football player, for a resident of a violent earthly kingdom at odds with his eternal citizenship. It is a must for a schemer and dreamer who thinks he's got the system beat and that the purpose of life is to facilitate acquisition of things and experiences for himself, things and experiences he hopes might make him whole.

* * *

As I left the safety net of a relatively wealthy home in which my teenage labor existed merely for character development and pocket money, I began to see clearly that I needed to "become other" than I was. Yet the existential questions remained, pressing harder and more deeply with each passing day. *What specifically was I to become? Also, how, to what end, and with whom?*

Section 3

On college

Chapter 13

What you've done becomes the judge of what you're going to do—
especially in other people's minds. When you're traveling, you are
what you are right there and then. People don't have your past to
hold against you. No yesterdays on the road.
William Least Heat Moon

The sunlight was fading into a glorious, breezy, late summer
evening as my parents' aging Toyota sedan disappeared around
the corner.

I stood there for a moment, then walked behind the building,
kicked my sandals off, and laid down in the grass. For 10
minutes, I lay there, holding in my hands the empty pillowcase I
would drool on the next four years, the empty pillowcase which
had fallen out of a box and my mom found at the last moment. I
lay staring at the painted sky and felt the cool grass between my
toes and held the pillowcase in my hands and considered for a
moment the weight and glory of what was before me.

Throughout my life to this point, I was defined, propelled,
and constrained by my own history and baggage. There was
never a point in my 18 years where I wasn't judged on the basis
of some part of my history. There was never a point in those 18
years where I wasn't known.

Frankly, I was tired, completely exhausted of being known
as – and tired of actually being – the person who was scared
to try. I was tired of being the kid who didn't know what they
wanted to be when they grew up. I was tired of being someone
who didn't quite stick out, but didn't quite have a place in an
enormous sea of a high school. I was tired of being the me I
had become and thrilled by the imagined opportunity to try
something new.

Though imperfectly, I was in the midst of one of those

rare moments in life where you start from close to zero. No familiarity, no job titles to seed division. New people, new perspective, and an opportunity – in extremely close-quarters with 35 complete strangers – for personal re-invention.

In this way, living on a freshmen hall is more than a bit like travel at its best. The isolation and disconnection from normalcy can be so intense and deep that it forces new relationships to take hold and new identities to emerge. In a very real sense, college was my first opportunity for this kind of formative travel.

When I walk up those stairs, I get to choose for myself how I will interact, how people will perceive me, who I will become.

And perhaps this is a choice we make every day. As holocaust survivor Victor Frankl said, "Man does not simply exist but always decides what his existence will be, what he will become in the next moment."

It wasn't that I wanted to be someone else, someone fake or superficial. Rather, I wanted to exist as a truer version of myself, someone freer, less constrained, more authentic.

I wanted to make great friends, and have magnificent adventures, and fall in love, and learn important things, and stay up too late, and play pranks, and get into trouble, but mostly escape unscathed. Above all, I was ready to have fun, lots and lots of fun for four years pretty much without ceasing and then leave this place changed and ready to be invisible and disconnected again in a new place, but with a better sense of who I was.

And so, I would.

In my enthusiasm, I forgot my sandals lying in the grass. I walked up those stairs, with earth still in my toes, holding the empty pillowcase that had fallen out of a box which my mom found at the last moment, and started a new life.

Chapter 14

We are playful when we engage others at the level of choice, when there is no telling in advance where our relationship with them will come out – when, in fact, no one has an outcome to be imposed on the relationship, apart from the decision to continue it.
James P. Carse, Finite and Infinite Games: A Vision of Life as Play and Possibility

Whenever my dad told stories from college, he always talked about pranks, chief among them that he hit some people in the face with pies for various reasons in public places. To me, this sounded hilarious and fun, but I needed to make the concept my own.

It all started with a guy I'll call "Shredder" from my hall. The day of his birthday in early October, I hit him in the face with a pie stolen from the cafeteria while my roommate filmed it and a shameful number of people looked on in awe.

The planning of the thing and the moments leading up to its execution were, perhaps sadly, amongst the most thrilling in my life. It was a genuine re-birth for me as my new identity (something a bit closer to authentic, or so I believed) began to take shape. Everyone involved – including Shredder, who was a great sport – also loved it. It was decided shortly thereafter that this event would become a tradition.

A few days later, Shredder posted a "hit list" of our hall's birthdays to my door, and the game was on.

The unspoken arrangement was that I had to get them on their actual birthday. That was the only rule.

I didn't miss a single person, and we got every one on tape.

We hit people coming out of the shower. We hit people on the IM Sports Field. We hit this one guy after hiding in his closet for nearly an hour waiting for him to enter his room. We hit someone a few weeks later at the library; got two other guys in the cafeteria; dropped a pie out of a window onto another guy's head. We even got a professor to hit my roommate with a pie at the end of class on his birthday.

This guy "Klossy" flipped one night before finals when I hit him as he entered the dorm. He grabbed the pie plate out of my hand after I smashed it in his face and somehow sliced my ear open in the process. We made up though. Years later, we'd tell this story amongst others in tear-filled speeches at each other's weddings.

Some others reacted or chased me, but most everyone just took it and laughed and shook their head at the camera.

On my birthday, the hall dragged me out of the building, tied me to a pole, and hit me with pie after pie after pie to get even.

It was our thing. One of many, in fact.

There was something beautiful and perfect about the shock factor and the clandestine nature of the thing. But what really helped it catch on was the communal aspect: the camaraderie, the knowing each of our times would come, the shameful amount of time we spent plotting each hit together and then re-watching in hysterical laughter.

It was also the common identity we gained from this and other hijinks. We were the hall that hit each other in the face with pies on their birthday and proved it with home videos.

From there it was easy for us to snowball our identity into something bigger. Starting in November, we became the group which led the Polar Bear Plunge – a near religious monthly ritual we maintained even when we had to start jumping through ice.

By December, we were the crew who had found the abandoned factory off-campus, led late night explorations of its every nook and cranny, climbed and rappelled off every rooftop and then started leading night tours to impress girls.

Chapter 14

Over Christmas break, we were the guys who came back early, found the lost entrance to the WWII era tunnels that crisscrossed the quad, and made it our mission to map these tunnels before graduation.

We were the hooligans who brought dilapidated go-karts back to campus for spring semester and rode with the wind in our faces in midnight time trials around a local park until we all got arrested. We were also the smooth operators who talked ourselves out of jail and got our chariot back from the 5-0.

We were the crazy guys. The ones who would think up something fun and unusual to do in subtle ironic revolt against authority or norms or maybe just the drab dullness of reality. We measured our victories in laughs, in epic stories, and in run-ins with the campus safety troupe as we embarked on an ever-escalating series of capers.

We were the crazy guys, and I was the ringleader, the instigator in chief.

But there was more to it than that.

* * *

There was an all-out Pennsylvania lake-effect blizzard that evening, some time in early January, and we were out in the thick of it. We'd spent the better part of the frigid evening on the dark, snow-blanketed lawn outside our dorm where, just a few months earlier, I'd lain with my feet in the grass and forgotten my sandals.

In those hours, we fashioned the finest makeshift dual-chamber igloo that Western Pennsylvania had ever seen. The rest of the night, we sat huddled inside, rejoicing at our creation and the good fortune of having found each other.

We were ecstatic with the possibilities of our own creative potential together. In those months of chaos and late-night adventures and a little bit of stressful studying, I think we were bonded by more than our love for mischief.

For the first time in any of our lives, we were living in the midst of a community of our own design. It wasn't the most perfect community. It didn't give us all the answers, and it certainly wasn't a model you could re-create everywhere or even somewhere else. It was particular to our situation and peculiar in all the ways each of us were.

Though we were all, in our own ways, living as individuals disconnected from our past, we were also part of building something beautiful and rich and complexly rooted in our own unique stories as much as in our common one.

Our hall was like the modern Church in that way, I think. The church is not some abstract ideal. It is not mere piety and holiness and perfected justice and Christ *fully* embodied on earth. Church, real church, is the church before us. The church that is present with us, the real people who call themselves by that name with all their problems and hang-ups. And it is amidst this broken, imperfect, striving, peculiar human church that we find our compass, our authentic purpose in this life.

It was amidst this church of sorts, this community, where I stumbled upon a growing ability to think deeply for myself and, through those thoughts, to learn about and love myself in spite of my brokenness. It was within this community where I learned – more slowly, more clumsily – to listen and learn from others, to hurt with them, and to grow with them in the tender moments where their journey intersected with my own. It was in my search for freedom and dislocation from my past that I stumbled into the presence of this community of people who shared certain things in common.

I will not suggest that all of these things were good and holy, but some of them were, and whatever it was that united us for those glorious months was real and powerful, at least for a time.

* * *

Driving back to school after spring break, I was completely beside myself with anticipation for what was to come.

Heroically, stupidly, whatever you want to call it, getting a good story was at the very core of our identity as a group. The written warnings from Campus Safety, the close encounters with actual law enforcement, the generally harmless menace we were becoming to the entire campus was all for the sake of the story.

In light of such an obviously timeless bond, I was certain our destiny was sealed. We would spend the next four years plotting a course of adventures and mishaps unlike any the school had seen. We would graduate by the skin of our teeth, and the school would enact a policy barring us or any of our offspring from ever again stepping foot on campus. Most importantly, we would be together.

But I was wrong.

That spring, my roommate and I decided to turn down an offer to join a fraternity and instead moved mountains to figure out a way for our core group of 10 to live on the same hall the following year.

In spite of this dramatic gesture of solidarity, the magic would never again be restored. As sophomores, our group became driven, called by other things, and left that thing which bonded us.

Just like all communities not built and continuously reaffirmed on the basis of something truly lasting, we fell apart. For some of us, school took precedent. For others, girlfriends came into the picture and created divides. Still others still grew tired of the endless seeking and striving for the next great story or felt more comfortable aligning themselves with more established, known groups across campus.

For one reason or another, we gradually drifted apart. These things happen, I know. But that year – those months on the IM field, on the "Time Trial" circuit, in jail cells, classrooms, and dorm rooms, the year plotting pie "hits" and other assorted mischief, the nights talking about life and growing close together – was special. I still sometimes think nostalgically about what might have been.

But alas, in the end, we proved the "magic" wasn't built on anything special or lasting. Today, I can claim but a single friend from that original group, and how "Klossy" even stuck is an unlikely story I'll save for later.

I pray it doesn't end the same way for our church of "resident aliens" as Stanley Hauerwas calls us in his eponymous classic. For this church is formed by something more core, more vital, than fun-filled nights in a Western Pennsylvania corn field or moments of emotive self-recognition huddled inside a deathtrap igloo.

Yet as a church, as a people, we don't necessarily behave that way. Indeed, we have gone far off base in our attempts to become the heroes of our own stories. We strive and fight and look for opportunities to re-make a world in our image, one in which we can take pride. We go looking for entertaining mischief or try to align ourselves with groups and systems we think might set us free, that might serve as substitutes for those things we crave most deeply – connection, love, belonging, truth.

But fortunately enough for me – and for us as a church – we don't have to be the heroes of our own story. We don't have to save ourselves.

"What we have first of all is not a heroic people, but a heroic God who refuses to abandon His creation, a God who keeps coming back, picking up the pieces, and continuing the story."

I had not yet recognized it, but this quote from Hauerwas' book characterizes my story, my conception of God, my experience with Him perfectly. After college I continued to stumble on, frequently forgetting my own story, seeking evermore opportunities for dislocated, immortal, heroic freedom from the chains of that finite, particular history. But a gradual awakening to a far deeper reality would soon begin to radically change the course of my life.

Chapter 15

It is remarkable that I am never quite clear about the motives for any of my decisions.
Dietrich Bonhoeffer – The Cost of Discipleship

Please don't get the wrong impression. There were plenty of shenanigans Sophomore Year and plenty more Campus Safety citations for my trophy wall. Frankly, I could easily fill many chapters with the stupid things I did that year.

But the crew was drifting apart, and the hijinks were more out of obligation for consistency with *what was* rather than sheer excitement for *what could be*. As with all disordered approximations of meaning, greater frequency and increasing intensity were required to reproduce that elusive plane which once set us "free."

Factory tours were an every weekend thing now. Fire extinguisher raids and impromptu dorm parties and nights spent sleeping outside in weird places around campus and other more normal modalities of college fun (i.e., beer and girls) were now part of my social DNA.

I was even, somehow, still hitting people in the face with pies. But this time, it was a business operation. That autumn, I made a dozen or so relatively high profile hits, all handsomely compensated.

At the end of the fall semester, even this, the old family trade on a grandiose scale, wasn't doing it for me. So, with little fanfare, PieMan retired, hanging up the mask and pie plate for good.

* * *

I couldn't fully articulate it at the time, but somewhere in my subconscious, I think I knew the *magic*, the real lasting thing behind all of the elaborate capers wasn't the novelty or the rebellious excitement of it all. It was the people, the release of control, of pretense, of self-consciousness and apprehension with people you love. No *next big thing* was going to resurrect what we had the year prior. And more than just "being together" I think I longed for a community which could be something more.

I wanted, in some small way, to play a part in building something which meant something.

Looking back, I see this as, truly, the earliest indicator of authentic longing for anything beyond my own personal glory. As with all glimmers of truth from broken humans, my idealistic intentions were certainly muddied by the reality of the ways in which I was choosing to live my life.

One day, I spoke to my old RA about these longings. Despite his knowledge of my reputation on campus, he suggested I consider becoming a freshman RA – leading a hall of freshmen men into their college experience.

Perhaps it's obvious at this point in the story, but such a vocation had never before crossed my mind. Yet, I felt strangely drawn to it.

I went ahead and applied, thinking, "Sure, I will be rejected out of hand." But I respected this guy and figured, *Why not?*

At the end of the application process, the Vice Provost for Student Life asked me to come to his office for a chat. I assumed this meant I'd somehow, against the odds, gotten the job and would be handed a batch of freshman guys the next year.

It wasn't quite that easy. I showed up at his office to find the VP sitting in his red leather chair next to none other than "Doug," my arch-nemesis, Head of Campus Safety.

In front of Doug lay a manila folder stuffed an inch thick with perforated forms. Across the top of the folder was written 645207, my student ID number.

"Jake, we liked the contents of your application, and some of our best ResLife staff have spoken highly of you as a strong potential leader," started the VP.

Doug grimaced and faintly smiled an evil campus safety-type smile and I knew there was a big *BUT* coming.

"But..."

There it was.

"This file contains your record of extracurricular encounters with Campus Safety..."

So that's the other half of those little paper trophies I'd been collecting.

"And the list of complaints and pending Campus Safety investigations where you are named as a prime suspect, but we've yet to be able to make a sufficient link."

Ohh... those ones.

"We have one of these files for every student on campus, and frankly, I've never seen one quite this, well, robust?"

We spent the next 30 or so minutes walking through each citation, complete with detailed explanation as to why each alleged offense was not the example they were hoping to inspire in a new cohort of students.

During the lecture, I had something of a realization that the little bursts of freedom and rebellion I had felt as I acquired those shenanigan trophies might just prevent me from doing something actually meaningful with the rest of my time on campus. For a moment, if just that, none of it really seemed worth it.

In the end – in perhaps one of the greatest lapses of judgment in college history – they decided to *probationally* accept me as a freshman RA under one explicit condition:

I would need to find an *approved* "upstanding citizen" to be my roommate – within two weeks.

This would be a challenge. I had a solid list of hooligans from my freshman hall who were ready to roll with me, but all of them either had a serious rap sheet themselves or were indirectly implicated by being part of "that crew."

To be honest, at this point in my life, I actually desperately needed a clean break.

Beneath all the fun and mischief and notoriety, I was drowning.

I was drowning in growing exhaustion with the expectations now set by my identity and reputation on campus.

I was drowning with resentment at my group who didn't share my vision for community or deeper union beyond the stunts and (increasingly alcohol-fueled) nights of mischief.

I was drowning in pain over a relationship with a girl which had developed and blown up and gotten the best of me at a time in my life when I thought I knew what love was, but really couldn't begin to understand such depth and meaning.

I was drowning in anger at myself for an inability to release my grasping for freedom and consistency and healing via human relationships which could never offer such lasting satisfaction.

Beneath it all, I was drowning.

Chapter 16

It's the people we hardly know, and not our closest friends, who will improve our lives most dramatically.
Meg Jay, The Defining Decade

Fast forward almost exactly two years from that conversation with Doug and the Vice Provost, and I'm floating weightlessly on my back just off Haiti's alluring Caribbean Coast. I look up at the clouds, allowing the beautiful, simple physics of salt and water and my particular BMI to cradle me on the gently rolling surface.

I reflect on everything that has transpired these last two years and how I'm now on a course I would have never expected.

I reflect on how a new community has been forming around me, lifting me up above the tugging undertow of life and opening my eyes to the realization of what the story of my life will ultimately be about.

I reflect on the clumsy ways in which I've attempted to pursue this new life and the lessons which are still only beginning to shape the way I look at the world.

I think back, to just a week ago, as my brave, stupid little group of guys crossed the overland border between the Dominican Republic and Haiti because the airport was shut down. We were there to be with a community leader who was trying to serve his people after a devastating earthquake.

I reflect on the infinitesimally small and possibly net-negative impact we had during our 10 days in-country, with our naivety and our utter lack of relevant skills. I ponder how and whether I might, some day, be able to contribute helpfully to such desperate situations. I question what it really looks like to "contribute" or "help" in a world so utterly, irreparably broken by the manifestations of our collective disordered quest for freedom and glory and power.

I wonder at the immeasurably complex and almost certainly net-negative impact of the broader western development-humanitarian industrial complex and the billions of wasted and misused dollars and diplomacy which largely serve to reinforce an oppressive system. I have a sliver of the beginning of a realization at how much pain my people have caused these people and others in the world, and it breaks me. I grieve the wide chasm that lies between humans, because of humans. Our ability to bring about healing through our own actions and plans seems impossibly out of reach.

I think, more hopefully now, about how my own life has been shaped and transformed by the undeserved love of a few men and women trying and failing to live out their own understanding of the ultimate meaning of this fleeting life.

I think of my friend Jeremy and his adventure which intersected with my own and led me to this moment. I think of my dear sister, Sarah, and her early, small, yet transformative engagements with the world beyond the US of A and the seeds her story planted in my own. Perhaps somewhere in there is an answer to all of these questions about how my life might do some good.

If only I could care about and invest in and love people like the main characters of my story, like Jeremy and Sarah and…

"JAKE!!!!!"

No, not Jake. Jake is still very stupid and ignorant. like…

"JAKE!!!!"

No, not Jake. Like, Bill.

"JAKE!!!!"

Wait. Is that Bill? Why is he screaming my name like that?

I snap out of it, moving to an upright position in the water, and try to get my bearings.

I'm still just 30–40 yards off-shore. Everything looks calm and peaceful. The other guys are still lounging on the beach. No sign of Bill.

"JAKE!!!!"

Bill's head re-surfaces above the water about 10 yards from where I'm at and he's clearly in trouble. Without thinking much further, I start swimming toward him.

I'm in front of him now, and he grabs me in sheer panic, pulling us both under the surface.

As I choke and pull water into my lungs, I realize I've made a serious mistake. I kick us back above the surface; using my free arm to pry his hand off and push him away, regaining control.

My long-since-expired lifeguard training finally kicks in, and I circle behind him to hold him up without giving him the opportunity to drown us both.

From this position, I talk to him as calmly as I can – though I'm sputtering salt water from my own lungs and growing dangerously tired. I tell him it's okay. I tell him he needs to lay flat in the water so I can swim us back to shore.

He's not listening.

I do my best to start swimming back and only then realize what's happened. We are in the middle of a very strong riptide. The shore is only 30 yards away, a 20-second swim for me were the water calm, but impossible to reach directly, and I don't have enough energy left to pull us both horizontally out of its grip.

I turn to the shore and see one of the other guys, "Gummel," walking along the edge, kicking shells aimlessly. Gummel, frankly, has been a major pain in the ass this entire trip and almost got us arrested at the border by being belligerent to a Haitian officer. I was questioning to myself earlier whether it was a mistake to bring him along.

Gummel is also, by mysterious grace, an All-American swimmer. I release Bill for a few seconds to wave frantically.

"HELP!! RIPTIDE!! BILL DROWNING!!"

His head pops up in my direction, but I'm not sure he's

heard.

I grab Bill as his head goes under the water again. My strength is leaving me, but I get him back up.

I pull and struggle to keep us level with the surface. We aren't going to make it back to shore on our own, but I can keep us above the water a little longer.

Bill's drowning, and I'm not going to leave him. He did the same for me once upon a time.

* * *

Two years prior, I had been desperate for a dependable roommate, and Bill was one of the best guys I knew. He was cool, but just dorky enough not to be totally full of himself, a rare trait in my group. He was hilarious and up for literally anything and had this amazing stubborn streak.

Bill's hall was right next to mine as freshmen and they also had a crazy reputation, if a little less on the "criminal underworld" side. One of the things they did for fun was to take turns open-palm slapping each other across the back. The idea was to go back and forth until one guy "won" when the other couldn't take it anymore.

Bill's hall was full of strong guys and natural athletes. Though he had his moments of awkward yet effective grace on the basketball court, Bill was not one of them. Yet Bill never lost the slapping game. He was feared, and many a guy from his hall wore his handprint on their back to prove it.

Bill was one of those guys who also cared intensely about everyone around him and drew others to himself through his goofy, endearing sincerity.

He was well aware of my reputation, and we weren't even all that close as sophomores. There was no chance in the world Bill would agree to live with me on a hall of freshman.

But Bill felt something, something faint and slippery and

beyond his comprehension or the finiteness of human logic. He somehow understood that I needed him that afternoon in April as we sat in my room, littered with beer cans and campus safety citations and the various other evidence of the misguided path toward "freedom" I was traveling.

Though he wouldn't use those words, he saw someone drowning, someone God might just have use for down the road, and he was there and he wasn't leaving.

Bill agreed to be my roommate and quickly became one of my closest friends, someone who could help me see what *just might* lie on the near shore of that ocean in which I was flailing around.

Bill was there. He held my head above water as I waited for someone stronger and more powerful to get me back to land and onto the path I would follow, albeit clumsily, for years to come.

* * *

I felt Gummel arrive before I saw him as he lifted much of Bill's weight from my grasp. Together, we fought and kicked our way out of the rip and desperately crawled and dragged Bill back to shore.

Finally, we collapsed there together exhausted, terrified, but alive with the tide sloshing harmlessly at our sides. I heard Gummel exhale something about that being the hardest thing he'd ever done in the water.

I had been able to hold Bill's head above water for a time, but alone we never stood a chance. In awe, I stared back up at that cerulean Caribbean sky and reflected on the immeasurable grace and mercy which had washed me up on this beach with these men.

Chapter 17

Invitation is not only a step in bringing people together, it is also a fundamental way of being in a community. It manifests the willingness to live in a collaborative way. This means that a future can be created without having to force or sell it or barter for it.
Peter Block, Community: The Structure of Belonging

With Bill on-board, the Vice Provost and Doug caved and decided to let us have our hall.

I don't believe my life had *a* particular turning point. It has been such a stumbling, back and forth sort of story. But something deep was beginning to change. It all started with Bill and the guys who rumbled onto that hall six months later.

From day one these freshmen guys breathed new life into my college experience – and more critically, my conceptions of community and leadership and "freedom." They opened my eyes for the first time to the greater adventure of surrendering my "right" to be "free" in exchange for the more binding, more gradual and uncertain process of learning to love a strange group of others.

Doing fun, stupid stuff is in my blood. That was going to happen. But our brand of fun was to be of a more subtle variety and a more intentionally communal one.

Instead of whipping pies in each other's faces, we were ever outside whipping discs back and forth, quietly building an unstoppable ultimate frisbee dynasty. Each season, we would make it to the IM Championships only to have our hearts crushed, usually in overtime.

We didn't have a polar bear club or sleep in igloos or rappel off factory roofs, but we did something almost as insane. Late in the fall semester, we developed a complex, nuanced "inside joke" manner of relating to each other based largely off a militant obsession with all things Latvian. One of the guys on our hall (we'll call him "Mr. Reds") had family from there and knew a good bit about the country. It kind of grew out of a celebration of this unique part of our collective make-up. But there was nothing rational about this "movement."

Somewhere along the road, we commissioned the painting of a large canvas portrait of "Mr. Reds" standing in a very Che Guevara-like pose in front of the Latvian flag. We dramatically named this painting "the colors" and paraded it around with us everywhere.

Several hall members learned every word of the Latvian national anthem. All members gathered to watch each match of the Latvian National Hockey Team and cheered them on with a socially inappropriate degree of vigor – often peppered with random Latvian swear words and colorful phrases at choice moments.

So fierce and unified was our devotion that it inspired interest in Latvia far beyond the core group. My senior year, a "Latvian Appreciation Club" was formed, and by the time my guys graduated, it boasted over one hundred members, many of whom were in high school when this inside joke first formed.

* * *

The spring of their senior year, I was attending grad school in the UK. One day in late April, I received a package in the mail with a postmark from my college town but with the sitting president of Latvia listed as the returnee. Three items were inside.

First was a note. It read:

"Sveiks *bruter Yak* (Hello Brother Yak — my "Latvian" name). Please find enclosed our most precious treasure, the honorable colors. We trust you will take her to her homeland where her heart truly lies. Find also our good news and great tidings from the home front. The faithful pure-blooded Latvians have finally found sweet victory on the IM battlefields over all Soviet imperialists. A symbol of our gratitude lies inside."

The second item was, of course, "the colors."

The third was a black T-shirt noting "A-League IM Championship Winners." The names of 11 guys from my hall were printed on the back, along with a twelfth who wasn't able to be in attendance: my own.

It was a week until their graduation. They had done it. Not all of them of course. Some had drifted apart, but the core group remained a community in just about the goofiest and weirdest way possible. Beneath it all ran a deep current of love.

I shook my head, opened my computer, and bought a ticket to Riga. The colors were going home.

* * *

I spent four days in the country later that year with none other than Mr. Reds. We stayed with his family, and I made him laugh with my persistent pretending to understand all the conversations in Latvian swirling around me. I waded into the frigid, filthy Daugava River with the colors in-hand, in defiant consummation of the most ridiculous inside joke I've ever had the privilege to participate in.

But it was more than an inside joke, a group obsession, or a sporting victory. It was a celebration of friendship by a group of people who recognized the language of love, but didn't know quite how to speak it just yet. In its place we lived together, played frisbee and everything else together, and spoke a demented, bastardized version of a Baltic language in a Western Pennsylvania corn field, together.

Chapter 18

If I were to wish for anything, I should not wish for wealth and power, but for the passionate sense of the potential, for the eye which, ever young and ardent, sees the possible. Pleasure disappoints, possibility never. And what wine is so sparkling, what so fragrant, what so intoxicating, as possibility!

Søren Kierkegaard, Either/Or: A Fragment of Life

The deep relationships which began to form my junior year were not just with Bill and the freshmen. That year, I had the decided privilege to live amongst a cohort of thoughtful, intelligent, loving fellow RAs who challenged me daily to be better than I was.

One of these guys invited me to come on a short trip to the Dominican Republic over spring break.

We were going there to build a bathroom or a wall or something for a Latin American satellite of a summer camp I had attended growing up.

At this camp and in other random chapters of my early life, I'd inexplicably become known as "Jeremy's other little brother" after a former counselor. It sounded like a good thing, but the name was usually evoked when I was breaking some rule or doing something crazy, so it was hard to tell.

Unlike my "older brother" whom I'd never actually met, I was rapidly approaching my twenty-first birthday and had never left the country. I didn't see much reason to do so, but the trip was really cheap and short, and I liked some of the folks who were going, so I went.

On day one, we arrived in Santo Domingo, DR, and I was overwhelmed – not the poverty, the smells, or the culture – but by the fact that you could buy delicious skewered meat right on the side of the road. You could stuff yourself for less than 50 cents.

That evening we rode in a big van out to the camp, and I blissfully brushed my teeth with the "fresh spring" tap water.

The next morning, I met some local kids who all bizarrely called me *Jeremito* or little Jeremy. These guys took me out for a swim in the lovely creek just downstream from the village, and I ate fruit off the trees and, per usual, didn't wash my hands much.

This is terribly heavy-handed foreshadowing: you can imagine what happened next.

"What happened next" was three days of laying in the sweltering heat in our open air bunkhouse running a high fever and puking my guts out every five minutes.

For the three days after that, I was too weak to do anything but wander around the camp like a pale ghost. I'd sit in the shade and sip on a Coca Cola while everyone else sweated away under the delusion that they were actually somehow helping these patient, skilled local workers. The workers themselves always seemed a bit nervous that some American kid was going to die on their watch.

Thinking back, this experience should have left scars and terrified me out of further flirtation with international travel, not to mention humanitarian work. But that's not really the effect it had. Neither the miserable days of sickness nor the patronizing unhelpfulness of the work we did are what first come to mind when I ponder that trip to the DR.

What I remember is riding with the Camp Director into town each day after the puking stopped to pick up more Coca Colas and supplies.

The Camp Director said I reminded him of "this Jeremy guy" he used to work with, and I guess he decided this was a good enough reason to let me tag along on his daily trip to town. I couldn't do much else, so I'd ride there and back standing in the bed of his truck with the wind and dust blowing in my hair, and I'd catch the feeling of freedom I'd long ago relished as a little boy.

From that privileged view, I got to see a tiny sliver of life the way most people lived it. For the first time, I began to realize, if not fully understand, that everyone didn't live life on the "pinnacle." And from that realization, that first real exposure to yawning inequality, I began to question. *What is the nature of our responsibility for this poverty, given how comfortable life is in the States, just a few hundred miles away?*

My interactions with the vibrant, joyful Dominican families I met also began an initial questioning and skepticism about the emptiness of rich world comforts, the loneliness of western material excess, the deep-seated fears and anxieties behind the quintessentially American illusion of safety and security. *We are far wealthier, but are we really better off?*

For me, it took a tangible experience – not quite a relationship, but at least a series of conversations with a few real people from the other side – for these questions to begin working their way into my heart.

It wasn't much, but this sliver-view was perhaps just enough – alongside Coca Cola made with real sugar and a taste of overland travel without pesky US-safety standards – to pique my interest and open my heart to a willingness, if not yet excitement, to do it again.

On day seven, we returned to Santo Domingo and flew back. To say I was "transformed" by the experience would be a massive overstatement. But as I returned to campus to figure out my summer plans, a seed had been planted.

* * *

That "figuring" process would turn out to be short and sweet. The day after arriving back in the states, I received a call from an old family friend who worked for an NGO. She was looking for an intern that summer and her top candidate had just pulled out. I had some other options in the hopper, but none which excited me.

With no conscious effort of my own, the preceding twelve months – through a Vice Provost's decision, a bad swimmer named Bill, a charismatic kid from Latvia, a rural family from the Dominican Republic, and an unexpected phone call – had radically reoriented my life in a direction I would have never anticipated.

Chapter 19

At all costs, figure out for yourself that life is not about how much you make, where you go, or what you do. It is not about doing everything in your power to stay alive as long as possible. The purpose of life is found in WHO you become. Live life with an open hand of surrender to what you cannot control.

Sean Litton, Former President, International Justice Mission

The summer after my junior year, I walked into the DC headquarters of International Justice Mission to commence my first real professional experience, an unpaid summer internship.

At the time, I knew next to nothing about IJM. Today, in humbling perspective, I am in awe of the transformation it has wrought on my life and the world we now occupy.

IJM is an organization dedicated to ending violent oppression against the world's poor. This oppression, as I would come to learn over the next months and years, is pervasive across the world in forms ranging from sexual abuse to land grabbing to labor exploitation.

IJM fights this status quo by working toward the reform of justice systems around the world – prosecuting cases, caring for victims, strengthening laws, policies, and institutions – so that they work more effectively for the benefit of the poor. IJM started from the vision and basement of its founder and excellent leader, Gary Haugen, and today has evolved into the world's largest anti-slavery organization.

* * *

Beyond the radical aspirations of this project, IJM is a unique organization because of the nature of its leadership and their posture of invitation for others to join in the beautiful story they are building with their lives.

Within two weeks, for example, Gary somehow knew every intern's name and began to develop real relationships with us. This wasn't just a short-term gimmick. Over the following 12 years, I'd return to IJM HQ for spontaneous visits and would occasionally run into Gary at various conferences or events. I was always touched when he recognized me by name, after I played such an insignificant role in the story of his organization. Eventually, I would accept an offer to re-join his team in my current role as IJM's Country Director in Cambodia, but I'm getting ahead of myself.

And it wasn't just Gary. Throughout that summer, IJM's senior staff generously made themselves available to share with us through brownbag lunches and other intern-focused events.

I remember (former IJM President) Sean Litton's talk as particularly formative.

Sean gave a 20-minute mini-lecture on "what to learn during your 20s." His points were simple.

At all costs, figure out for yourself that life is not about how much you make, where you go, or what you do.

I noticed some uncomfortable seat-shifting at this first point.

These interns were people my age who were already *doing things* and pretty much seemed like they knew *where they were going*. They had started businesses and charities, lived overseas, thought through big issues, and had developed, to varying degrees, well-constructed plans for how to climb whichever ladder they so desired.

I'd later discover there were more than 500 applicants for the 14 coveted (again, unpaid) summer jobs. I slipped in through the cracks via a fluke of timing, the privilege of connection, and parents who lived in the area.

Suffice to say, a 21-year-old mischief-maker like me had no business being there. My middling grades, my 7 days of cumulative international experience (mostly spent puking in a bunkhouse), and my utter lack of professional expertise (gambling, landscaping, life-guarding) put me well below standard for IJM's intern class.

Nonetheless, I was beginning to feel the early whispers of ambition defined more specifically than vaguely desired immortality; that internal drive to *do things* and be defined by that *doing*. This summer was to be the busiest period yet in my life – working the internship, taking Calculus online, and training for my first marathon in the sticky northern Virginia heat.

So, yeah. Sean's first point was de-stabilizing for me as well.

It is not about doing everything in your power to stay alive as long as possible.

Material pursuits imply a driving desire to stick around long enough to enjoy the top. When you abandon such fearful clinging to life altogether, it opens up a whole new range of options on how to live.

A few weeks later, Sean invited his good friend Dave Eubank to speak to our class. Dave was an ex-Special Forces Officer and leader of a paramilitary humanitarian group called the Free Burma Rangers (FBR).

Dave and his team had found a calling which pushed them far beyond a preoccupation with personal safety or the quintessentially American illusion of security.

FBR's *thing* was to sneak across Myanmar's closed border to offer support to internally displaced villagers. These villagers were trying to survive constant attacks from a military-controlled government which had blocked access to the country for all humanitarian groups.

This mission and outlook on life struck a chord with me. A year later, I would find myself working for Dave in that jungle, but, again, I'm getting ahead of myself.

Sean's next point was the one that really hit me in that moment and lies at the core of how I've tried (and frequently failed) to posture my life ever since.

The purpose of life is found in WHO you become. Live life with an open hand of surrender to what you cannot control.

In recent years, I've spent time amongst some of the top leaders, brightest minds, and most influential thinkers in my field. Yet, never have I found myself so much in awe of the brilliance, humility, and passion exhibited by those around me as in that summer internship. This is much more a statement about their *who* than their *what, where,* or *how much.*

These were a people long immersed in a community of purpose, one which put them in contact with the world's most vulnerable at a proximity and frequency far beyond the norm in our society. In so doing, they had learned – or were quickly learning – to make others the hero of the story, instead of themselves. The difference was visible. Their *who* had gained immeasurably by this surrender.

Those three months at IJM, I was bombarded daily by contact with intelligent, accomplished, humble leaders – not to mention exposure to a compelling mission. These folks were willing, seemingly eager, to pour into my life. In so doing, they – always gently, but almost forcibly – opened my eyes to a new way of viewing the world and my place in it.

But, none so much as Jeremy Shull.

* * *

It was 6:30pm on a Friday afternoon in May 2009. I was boarding the elevator which would take me to IJM HQ for the first time. Nearly 50 staff had volunteered to host a welcome party for the new intern class as a start to their weekend.

I was a few minutes late and so was he, this IJM employee who looked like he might, in another life, be my brother.

"Hi, you must be one of our new interns! My name is Jeremy."

When Jeremy and I finally met, his reputation had preceded

him, and our friendship was already well underway. To borrow his words from a few years later, "I felt a sense of deep understanding as you can only have with someone pressed from the same mold."

The sheer number of shared experiences, just-barely-missed paths crossed, overlapping interests, and ridiculously similar shenanigans and stories were uncanny. From Northern VA to a summer camp in Pennsylvania to the DR to our strange, mutual choice in college where we captained the Rugby team – amongst too many more to list – our lives had unknowingly mirrored one another in parallel decades.

Far beyond such surface-level "coincidences," I quickly found in Jeremy a more mature, more thoughtful version of my own adventurous soul. Our struggles, our hang-ups, our hurts, our brokenness as well as our loves, our passions, our strengths, were deeply intertwined, if only more developed in him.

The more I got to know Jeremy, the more I realized that not only had I found the "older me" in many ways, but I'd also found the best version of my future self, the man I wanted to become.

As I reflect over the past decade, I find my life shaped and guided by his presence as a mentor and a brother, one of few people who could consistently speak into my life with truth and love and authority. It is not an overstatement to say that every good, healthy, positive decision I made from that moment as a rising senior to this day was and is influenced by the life Jeremy lived and the ways in which he welcomed me into his story.

The rest of this book is littered with moments where Jeremy saved or dramatically changed my life for the better through the direct guidance or indirect influence of his soft words, courageous instincts, and strong character.

* * *

Years later, in the run-up to my wedding date, I started getting cold feet as young men are prone to do. I longed for "freedom" to explore the corners of the earth and climb every mountain and do everything I didn't yet know I wanted to do – *and how could I possibly do all these great things in the face of all the pain which comes from being tied to another?*

Naturally, Jeremy was the first person to whom I turned.

He challenged me – as he once did in a similar crisis of confidence – to take some time by myself in the Colorado wilderness which beckoned us both so irresistibly. He encouraged me to think and write and pray and reflect on *who* I wanted to become.

I was delighted by the idea and by the knowledge, that once again, Jeremy had gone there first and that I was, in a sense, walking in his footsteps in this great adventure of life.

The night I left for my time of meditation, I received a letter with no return address and no signature, though the postmark was from Jeremy's hometown and the handwriting was unmistakable, eerily similar to my own. In the envelope was a single quote, which defines for me Jeremy's approach to life and love:

So, if he wanted the heights of joy, he must have, if he could find it, a great love. But in the books again, great joy through love seemed always to go hand in hand with frightful pain. Still, he thought, looking out across the meadow, still, the joy would be worth the pain – if, indeed, they went together. If there were a choice – and he suspected there was – a choice between, on the one hand, the heights and the depths and, on the other hand, some sort of safe, cautious middle way, he, for one, here and now, chose the heights and the depths.

The quote, from Sheldon Vanauken's *A Severe Mercy*, spoke to my uncertainty, fear, and doubt. It beckoned me to open my hands; to release my endless pursuit of supposed "freedom" which had so controlled and bound me throughout my life. It challenged me to surrender fully to that great adventure we call love.

In this quote, in this terribly direct, but also mysterious way of giving advice, I felt Jeremy's deep understanding of the beautiful and contingent nature of life, that it wasn't a question of *what, where,* or *how much,* but *who* – and perhaps, *who* is there beside you.

In his pursuit of life and love, he lacked the illusions of safety, security, and control which plague most.

He desired to face life with open hands and an open heart and by desiring such a posture for me, helped me walk through the most important (and best) decision of my life.

We don't all get a role model like that, and I miss mine deeply.

Chapter 20

The only thing I see as distinctly different about me is that I am not afraid to die on the treadmill.
Will Smith

Something was changing as I returned to campus that fall.

Maybe it was the experience at IJM and Jeremy's growing influence. Or perhaps it was merely the changes in brain chemistry which occur when you train for a marathon in Virginia's swampy, late-summer heat.

Regardless, I was beginning to approach my life in every aspect – from college pranks to school to job search to athletics – with an intensity, purpose, and drive I'd never before felt.

I still didn't know exactly what I wanted to be when I grew up (nor do I today), but all of a sudden, I had something to prove. Not to anyone in particular, but to myself. For twenty-one and a half years, I'd more or less drifted through life and now, suddenly, I was awakened to a fire burning within me.

* * *

Preparations for my first 26.2 mile run both fueled and exemplified this newfound internal flame. I had trained with dedication. I had tapered intelligently and felt strong as the day approached. I had analyzed my fitness accurately and had a reasonable goal pace in mind.

Race day, the weather was perfect – a typically crisp, cool mid-October morning in the nation's capital. I felt healthy and rested. I had carbo-loaded. It was time for the new and improved me to be unveiled to the world.

As it had been for my entire sheltered American life, everything seemed perfect for my first marathon. Inputs had always equaled outputs, and I had put in the work, so I felt assured of success.

One variable though, lay entirely beyond my control: I had trained with water bottles. The race supplied paper cups.

In training, I would lay out bottles of water and Gatorade every 3–4 miles, and that had always been sufficient.

Grabbing a tiny cone cup of Gatorade at miles 4, 8, and 12 didn't faze me, and somehow, I didn't think about how much less, how *dramatically* much less, I was drinking.

Amongst endurance athletes, the "wall" is a term thrown around to describe the feeling of complete mental, emotional, and physical agony that you run into near the end of a race. In most well-trained, well-paced runners, this happens around mile 21–24 when the body uses up the last of its carbohydrate reserves and starts having to burn fat for fuel. Those last few miles are pure hell, and the "wall" is where the true mental test of the marathon begins.

Also commonly known amongst marathoners is the fact that the wall can move itself *significantly* forward if you pace too quickly or don't consume enough calories, or say, drink barely any water.

I hit the wall at mile 13.

At that point, I'd been running for nearly an hour and a half at about the right pace for my level of fitness at the time. I had, however, consumed less than 8 ounces of Gatorade and was hoping to keep that pace for another 13-ish miles.

It struck me that I was feeling miserable, but it did not strike me that I needed to start drinking more. I just kind of figured this was what marathon running was going to be like for me.

Something else happened at mile 13. It was something I hadn't felt in nearly 10 years since that moment running the track at my middle school jog-a-thon. Something clicked in my head and told me I couldn't stop, wouldn't stop.

Remember, a ridiculous tolerance for race threshold pain

was one of my great gifts.

But that first encounter with agony had been 10 years earlier, 9 years and 8 months of which I had decidedly not spent training for this moment. There would be no miracles.

My stubbornness nonetheless remained intact, and walking was not deemed an option.

It took nearly 2 hours to shuffle-jog the second half of that race, my pace slowing to an agonizing crawl. But I never walked.

I kept telling myself, lying to myself, that I'd run to the next aid station, the next mile marker, the next corner, the next 10 steps, and then take a break, but I never did.

I kept telling myself, lying to myself that it mattered, that not walking, not bending to the excruciating pain would tell me something important or lasting about myself. I was convinced (or at least trying to convince myself) that leaning into that suffering would somehow momentarily quench the fire now burning in my soul – that it would set me "free" – if only for a moment.

I collapsed just across the finish line, puked, and then blacked out. I woke up with an IV in my arm. I think I consumed approximately 16 ounces of water or about a normal-sized water bottle over the course of the entire 26.2 miles and had lost almost 10% of my body weight.

It was neither a healthy nor recommended first marathon experience, but it somehow shook loose a recognition of a deep truth for me. It is embarrassing for me to admit, but in nearly 21 years, that moment, those hours of agony, were my first true realization that the world is not fair; that I won't necessarily get what I think I deserve just because I work for it; that hard, committed work and goals have their own reward even if, especially if, the outcomes remain unknown and perhaps just out of reach.

* * *

A decade on, I've completed several dozen marathons on 5 continents and counting; a number of ultra-distance trail runs including a Grand Canyon Rim2Rim run; and an IronMan Triathlon, amongst other grueling physical endeavors.

Yet, that first marathon in my youth and in perfect weather on a flat course in my hometown remains ingrained in my memory as the most difficult and miserable race, the greatest self-inflicted pain of my life.

It also stands as a recurring reminder to someone all too often driven by an avoidance of pain – a deep, disordered yearning to be "free" from it – just how truly liberating it can be to step into the unknown, and fail.

Chapter 21

There are deeper reasons to travel – itches and tickles on the underbelly of the unconscious mind. We go where we need to go, and then try to figure out what we're doing there.
Eleanor Roosevelt

Everything was always going to be different as I began to stumble uncertainly down a new path after that summer at IJM and an autumn of awakening to the hope and possibility which can arise from suffering and failure.

But then – for a brief moment – all of life seemed strangely familiar.

Senior year, I lived with five of my freshman guys from the previous year in the university's largest room. It was called the "palace."

At the time, the name felt justified. Today, I would call it what it was: six dudes living in a crappy 2-bedroom apartment adjacent the pool and gym.

Location is everything though, and we took full advantage of ours at the heart of campus. The palace served as a hub for a bit of the hooligan behavior I'd indulged in freshman and sophomore years, though we were operating at a higher level by this point.

Fall semester was all about planning – constructing something of a speakeasy in the drop ceiling above our room and cutting through the rebar separating our ceiling from the one above the pool. Spring was all about execution – hosting parties and "cliff diving" the 30 feet to the chlorinated waters below.

Outside the room itself, my "extracurricular activities" centered on a self-appointed responsibility to wield an industrial grade megaphone. Heckling couples making out around campus and narrating/directing the misdeeds of an army of full body animal costumes was basically a full-time job which I took very seriously.

And that was pretty much my senior year in a nutshell.

Except it wasn't.

* * *

Alongside fervently trying to squeeze the very most out of my college experience, I was also desperately seeking an avenue to continue down the unclear, yet alluring path started that summer at IJM.

Initially, the "plan" had been to pursue a normal Accounting career upon graduation. After all, I had chosen Accounting as a major primarily because of how easy getting a job was supposed to be.

I applied to the "Big Four" and received an offer from one. With no other legitimate options in sight, it seemed like this was to be my life.

I should have been learning about the organization and the role of an auditor. I should have been studying for the dreaded CPA exam. I should have been getting ready to be an accountant.

Nothing was further from my mind.

* * *

At that point, Jeremy and I were talking weekly over the phone about his experience doing relief work in Haiti. Jeremy had a friend there who was asking him to return to Haiti to help with some projects.

Jeremy couldn't go this time, but he asked if I wanted to try to lead a group from college.

I'd get to visit a new country and learn about their situation and potentially expose some of my friends to international travel, something I was realizing held a strange, potentially transformative allure for me.

I was in.

I did a bit of recruiting and cobbled together a group of four brave and stupid guys willing to follow me to the poorest country in the hemisphere.

As the fall semester drew to a close, we prepared to buy our tickets for spring break – the first week of March.

Then, on January 12, 2010, a catastrophic earthquake rocked Port-au-Prince, shutting down the airport and plunging the country into chaos.

Word came from our host a few days later: if we could still make it, the need was even greater than before. We'd just need to come in via the Dominican Republic and meet him at the bus station in Cap Haitian (the northern city).

From my perspective, this didn't pose a problem. I "knew" the DR and "spoke Spanish" so navigating the voyage shouldn't be an issue.

The guys agreed with this logic, somehow.

And so it came to be that a 21-year-old with no international experience, technical expertise, or language skills led a largely independent, overland multi-country relief trip, 5 weeks after the largest natural disaster of the preceding decade into a deeply impoverished country rapidly descending into anarchy.

* * *

There we were, sitting at the bus station ready to leave the "safe" country on the island. The last 16 hours had felt anything but safe. During that first brief foray "leading" "humanitarian" "work" (all quotes totally necessary) we: arrived several hours before dawn and decided to walk the 4 miles to the bus station in the absence of having arranged a driver; were chased by crazy dogs multiple times and held at gunpoint once while wandering completely lost in vague route to said bus station;

boarded the correct bus and rode a mile before deboarding in a panic believing it to be the wrong one due to my poor grasp of Dominican Spanish; waited an additional six hours at this sweltering, putrid-smelling bus station for attempt #2; and had absolutely nothing to eat in this entirely unfamiliar foreign country.

Self-inflicted mishaps aside, we had, miraculously, succeeded with step one: make it to the bus in time. In the process, an incredible sense of uncertainty had overtaken me. This was the least certain I had ever been of my own physical safety; my cavalier, naive confidence stripped to the bone.

More frightening still, I am sitting with three other guys who are looking to me for direction and I am asking them to board that bus. That bus is headed straight across the notoriously corrupt DR/Haitian border into the most chaotic country in the western hemisphere. The end goal in all of this is to work with a local community leader to whom I now realize we will offer no true help and who I am sure these guys doubt even exists. I have absolutely no idea if he will show up at the bus station and even less of an idea what we will do if he doesn't.

I am in way over my head. And this was supposed to be the easy country.

* * *

For 22 years in the US, I had never been in a situation where I felt so entirely out of control, so utterly at the mercy of whatever ends up happening.

Suddenly this realization struck me. Just as quickly the inherent craziness, stupidity, and emptiness of a life confined to such an illusory bubble struck me as well.

In less than a day on my own in the DR, I was stripped bare of the façade of control to which I had long clung. My eyes were abruptly forced open to the reality of a life which demanded

I put my faith, my security, and my will in a power beyond myself. I would need to repeat this process of surrender again and again in the coming years, as I often forgot to walk in light of that reality, but the seal was broken that day.

Amidst this storm of chaos, I felt strangely at peace.

We boarded the bus.

* * *

If my first visit to the Dominican Republic opened my eyes to another world and a new path, Haiti beckoned and pulled me in like a tractor beam.

I didn't have any clue *what* I would do, but I certainly knew *that* I would do *it*.

I was moved by the poverty, by the beginning of an understanding of what it looks like when entire systems are not functioning for the people who need them most.

More than that though, I was moved by the minor, temporary transformation which overcame *me* when *I* was forced out of *my* American bubble. *I* was inspired by the feeling of freedom *I* felt from the chains of *my* own illusion of control. *I* was somehow changed by the experience of living outside the known.

Almost overnight, I became driven to do something, anything, everything else which might re-create that feeling.

It wasn't like I was floating in options after graduation either. I had one. By the books (pun intended), my audit job at Deloitte was a really good one.

Against the weight of my newfound excitement for transformation via experience, it never stood a chance.

With less than three weeks to graduation, I declined my only offer of gainful employment.

Chapter 22

In the presence of nature, a wild delight runs through a man, in spite of real sorrows. Nature says, – he is my creature, and maugre all his impertinent griefs, he shall be glad with me.
Ralph Waldo Emerson

Suburban, mainstream, white-collar America is not a place I typically look for stories of courage and true, acted upon faith. The self-reinforcing temptations inherent in this world make it an easy target for critics of the privileged, sheltered, safety-clinging American life.

For me though, the stereotype blew up the week my parents decided my dad should quit his job.

The decision itself, the whole "bravely walking away from a good job" thing as I edged ever nearer to the void beyond graduation was made easy by the example of my parents. My dad had slaved away in DC for 17 years as an IT consulting beltway bandit with the obligatory 90-minute commute each way while my mom held down the full-time job of keeping us alive.

Earlier that year, they both felt a call. Not the call of adventure or excitement or a better quality of life, but an actual call – with a kid in college, a mortgage, at the peak of his career and at the first moment of rest for her in over two decades – that they needed to walk away from their bubble of perceived safety and control.

For me, this was an authentic, inspiring example. *If they could make such a decision with so much (perceived) to lose, why shouldn't I take a risk?*

Several months later, Dad found a job at Compassion International. As fate (and a heavy dose of privilege) would have it, I was accepted to an internship at Compassion the very same week.

My motives were less pure, my risk less truly risky. Nonetheless, like every good decision I've ever stumbled into, I did it following a better, bolder, purer example.

In the end I turned down the big-name Accounting firm and the safe, wealthy, depressing life I thought it promised and instead accepted an offer for a three month, part-time $8/hour internship in Colorado Springs. After a few more weeks with my crew, I graduated and drove across the country to start a new, uncertain life.

* * *

The first day I walked through those doors at Compassion, I met my best friend and my wife, Rachel. I wouldn't know it for another year and a half, and it wouldn't be true for another nearly three years, but if ever there were a day which changed my life, this was it. That's a story for another time. We were just friends that summer after all.

The day I met Rachel, I also met the mountains, and that one *was* love at first sight. I had been in the mountains before, but only to ski at resorts. This summer would change all that.

Resort skiing is a thrill-seeking, voyeuristic activity like dirt biking and ATV riding and off-roading. You are propelled on your journey by another force. As such, you fail to fully recognize the gravity of that experience. The ascending journey is an ignored, passing thing. It's what you do so you can come back down.

In a resort, you are offered a marketed version of a spectacular reality. It's like a drive up to the South Rim of the Grand Canyon or through the mighty Redwoods on Route 101 without further exploration of the deeper mysteries within.

Engaging in such activities, I never really feel like I'm *in* the mountains, but rather passing through them, experiencing the majesty of nature, but not really meeting it. I'm not really being changed by it. I risk nothing and thus, I don't really begin to *know*.

Only by traveling through something on my own finite power, only upon re-remembering my own fragility and impermanence amidst utter grandeur do I ever really begin to know it and be formed by it.

Almost overnight, hiking, climbing, mountain biking, trail running, kayaking, and backcountry skiing became a sort of spiritual experience for me. In a deep way, each venture into the wilderness recalls for me a certain, important element of my early international experience.

For me, it all comes back to the gift outdoor adventures offer us to escape our modern bubble of controlled outcomes and selfish ambitions in re-recognition of the true nature of reality.

Staring hundreds of feet straight up at the fragile, verdant redwood giants who have stood in quiet watch amidst these ferns for centuries – and are now threatened by the daily decisions of our society – is a reminder of our responsibility to this deeper reality.

Succumbing to the heat and distance and sheer vertical insanity on the north rim of the world's largest canyon will realign even the most self-assured human with what a fragile, impermanent role we truly play in the cosmos.

Released from our delusions, such moments can help us remember our true selves as tiny and insignificant and stumbling beings striving destructively after meaning amidst and often against the tide of a great and beautiful story beyond our reckoning.

In a very real sense, this is the story of my relationship with Rachel. In fact, I often think of human love in such terms. A beautiful release of control, a willingness to see yourself as insignificant, intertwined, and along for the ride of whatever winding, unknowable story is at play in the life of another.

What more can we gain from this life than through the ultimate risk of giving ourselves fully to another broken human?

I was not yet ready for such a journey, but I would stumble upon it eventually, wandering the endless paths through these mountains and others.

* * *

By the end of that summer, I knew at least one path I was to follow, and that was an initial exploration of a life abroad. One day in late July, as the internship drew to a close, a conversation with a Compassion colleague reminded me of Free Burma Rangers, that under-the-radar humanitarian organization I'd encountered a year prior.

I had the Director's business card and sent him a note inquiring about availabilities for employment. I guess there wasn't huge interest in running around war zones because he responded with an application, and then, a week after I submitted it, invited me to join. The job was for a Logistics and Reporting Officer based in FBR's HQ in Chiang Mai, Thailand. I would learn about Human Rights reporting and advocacy, create a database of FBR's reports, and help plan and prepare for relief missions.

That same day, I called up Jeremy to see what he thought. Of course he said I should do it. Turns out, one of Jeremy's friends, a fellow named Matt, was also over there working for Harvard Human Rights Clinic and Amnesty International. Jeremy said we'd get along and made the connection. Matt responded the next day, graciously offering his couch until I found a place to stay and a spot as a Research Assistant on his project.

It was a two-part first job combo beyond my wildest dreams. The next day, I bought a one-way flight to Thailand and began stumbling down the next section of my path.

But first, I had to say goodbye.

Chapter 23

We were promised sufferings. They were part of the program. We were even told, 'Blessed are they that mourn,' and I accept it. I've got nothing that I hadn't bargained for. Of course it is different when the thing happens to oneself, not to others, and in reality, not imagination.

C.S. Lewis, A Grief Observed

Before taking off for Thailand, I spent a long weekend in Pennsylvania to say goodbye to my friends at school and help my sister kick-off her junior year.

Sitting on a plane, I caught my breath for a moment at the journey I'd traveled those last 12 months. From a glance, not too much had changed.

I was training for another marathon and making another long haul out to school. I was finishing off another uniquely challenging summer, with another new opportunity to explore just around the corner. Another gaping question mark loomed about a year down the road.

As I looked closer though, the similarities began to fade.

Flipping through my training log, I realized my workouts were stronger than they were a year earlier. Apparently, a summer at 7,000 feet and dedicated training for two marathons the previous season had made me faster.

I was back at school, but in an entirely different way. Never again would I walk these halls as a student. I returned for a brief trip to move my sister in and visit some old friends.

Twelve months earlier, my life was here in this Pennsylvania cornfield – my personal epicenter of familiarity, friends, and immense comfort. This time, it took me to the other side of the globe, away from everything I knew.

Last year, I was just beginning to gain a curiosity for life outside my comfort zone. A yearlong introduction to such situations left me totally addicted to a radical new way of living.

That abyss waiting at the end of my senior year – the unknown and the unknowing – scared the hell out of me. This year, it motivated and beckoned me to live life more fully, to live it with an open hand, surrendering to what lay beyond.

* * *

That weekend, I said goodbye to three of my closest friends and essentially closed the chapter which was the first 22 years of my life. Being a kid was awesome, but I got the sense that my carefree weekend bumming around campus marked an end to that era. From the moment I walked onto the quad, a voice inside me screamed, "You don't belong here anymore!"

I tend to think it was referring to more than just the college campus.

Recognizing the end of my childhood and moving on with grace was just one more challenge which awaited during the crazy upcoming stint in Southeast Asia. The entire experience would test me in ways I could not yet imagine.

Surprisingly, fear was never one of the emotions I felt leading up to my departure, until the moment I began to say goodbye, that is.

"Are you worried about going to Thailand?"

"What are you most apprehensive about?"

"It's going to be so different. Aren't you scared?"

My answer to these common questions was quite insufficient, as I couldn't think of anything which truly scared me. I mean, I was (and am) terrified of snakes, but I'm not sure that's what they meant. Snakes are everywhere, you know.

Really, truly though, nothing about the adventure was keeping me up at night. Excited? Yes. Scared? Not really.

Everything changed that night when I started saying

goodbye. Separation from the comfort of familiar people didn't bother me. Again, I was excited about this challenge and the new opportunities for fellowship it would bring.

Saying goodbye to my sister, a comrade since birth, was a totally different story. Never before had we been so completely separated, and our goodbye remains one of the toughest things I've ever had to do.

Immediately following this painful farewell, I had to do it all over again. Bill entered my life at its darkest point and was a major part of helping me turn things around. I shudder to think what my life would look like today without his faithful friendship.

A week later, it was another kind of goodbye. Rachel was now working full-time at Compassion. She agreed to meet me at a cheap Mexican grill, and she ordered a crappy cheese quesadilla if I remember correctly.

That summer we were just friends, and I was pretty sure it would never be anything more. But sitting there in the decaying bench amidst food which was certainly not FDA-certifiably safe, I couldn't help wonder, but, what if? So, before we hugged our platonic friend hug goodbye, I got her new email address and an agreement to stay in touch.

Perhaps these goodbyes didn't need to be forever.

As I drove to the airport, I realized how different everything was going to be and reflected again on the question of fear as I embraced this new path. Not just in Thailand and Myanmar, but for the rest of my life.

The era of home and school and college, in which the people I cared about were easily accessible, was over. Sure, I could still keep in touch with a few and someday hope to start a family of my own, but from then on, relationships were going to require much more intentionality, commitment, sacrifice.

And well, I was pretty scared about that.

* * *

Six months later, it's a rare peaceful, sunny afternoon on a usually rainy, usually war-torn hilltop in Northern Myanmar when I break down for the first time on my new life path.

This is a different kind of goodbye.

These last months introduced me to the imminent reality and the deep sadness of death. This journey brought me closer to the dead and dying and at a greater frequency than most Americans will ever experience. This exposure shook something loose in me, ultimately transforming the way I view and approach life. But this death, over 10,000 miles away, was different, closer somehow.

My family is all together now, minus two key people. One of them is me.

I was the first grandson and for 20 months thrived as the sole treasure of the family. Then Andrew was born. Even before my sister, Andrew was my first playmate. He was a meaningful part of my every memory with Mom's side of the family tree.

Most of our interactions took place at the "farm," my grandfather's yawning plot of west Texas clay. My visits to the farm were often separated by large periods of time, gaps which grew in length as the years wore on. Proximity ultimately stifled the full development of our friendship, but I always considered Andrew the closest thing I had to a brother.

Andrew lived near the farm, and every month my family would visit. We would always pick up right where we left off: exploring the fields, playing hide n' go seek in the farmhouse, trying for hours just to get a single ball through the towering, rusty, old basketball net.

As time passed, the monthly trips turned into every few months, but the fun only increased as my sister and his brother joined the ranks: camping in the fields, building a fortress in the barn, throwing apples at the cows, two-on-two at the rusty, old basketball net.

Then we moved north and only made it out to the farm a couple of times a year. But whenever we did, everything was beautifully unchanged. Our club of cousins really was family: 4 wheeling around the fields, fishing by the tank, climbing races to the top of the rusty, old basketball net.

But twice a year turned to once, and once to "when we can," and the assembly of our childhood army lost its regularity. Nearly two years had passed when I headed back to the farm for Pappaw's funeral. A fifth cousin, Andrew's youngest brother, had long been added to the ranks and was now 6 years old. Somewhere along the way, we had all grown up, Andrew perhaps the most visibly.

During Pappaw's final days, Andrew had grown into a leader at the farm and in life. He was excelling at university and prepping for law school (a veritable family tradition). At home, he was looking after his brothers and spending a lot of time with a special girl named Ashley.

That summer he had stopped by the old house every day to check in on Mammaw and Pappaw. Whether to bring them the mail, or deliver some groceries, or just to say hi, he was there. The farm became just another place where he could make a difference: plowing the fields, taking care of the cows, thoughtfully repainting the rusty old basketball net.

I was thoroughly impressed by the changes in Andrew's life, changes I was actively seeking in my own. Though time certainly forced its way between us, the friendship was just as we remembered.

I'll never forget a moment we shared on my last trip to the farm. Andrew and I were worn out from spending an hour or so trying to dunk on this refinished – yet unmistakably old – basketball net (I never quite got it, but I think he did). We headed around the house and met the other three cousins. The five of us just sat there under the flag, tossing a football, and enjoying each other's company for the rest of the afternoon. I couldn't stop thinking to myself how lucky I was to have such a family, so separated by time and distance, but still – in many ways – so beautifully close.

As the sun set, we hugged our goodbyes and headed back to school and life on opposite sides of the world. That was the last time I heard from Andrew.

* * *

There I sat, alone and confused on this hillside in Northern Myanmar, seeking in this strange land the sort of personal transformation which became real for Andrew in his own home town.

My family was all together, minus two key people. One of them was me.

Section 4

On exploration

Chapter 24

If you reject the food, ignore the customs, fear the religion and avoid the people, you might better stay at home.
James Michener

110° F and 100% humidity soak my T-shirt in the first 10 minutes outside, but I barely notice. I'm overcome by all the other sensations. I encounter a new smell every block, and they all overpower me. I've never seen so many taxis going so many different directions in my life. I've never heard so many noises so loudly.

And it is all just noise to me.

Spanish carried with it some familiarity – if not true understanding – but this is different. I notice the lack of Roman characters from the billboards, replaced by indecipherable Thai symbols. There is something very isolating about not even recognizing words as such.

Only in the food do I find a seemingly universal connection. Come to think of it, my tongue has been on fire for the last hour.

I'm walking through the streets of Bangkok, and every sense screams at the visceral newness. This is the largest city I've ever encountered. Right now, I might as well be on another planet.

It is my first day in Thailand, coincidentally just a day before the second round of the 2010 red shirt rallies. The first round, spawned by political unrest a few months prior, rocked the country and drew international attention when 85 protesters were killed by police. Today is the political calm before the storm as the city braces itself for the unknown. The second round turned out to be uneventful, but you wouldn't guess it by the weather today.

I would normally be running for cover because the bottom just dropped out of the sky. But really, with no poncho and over a mile to go, what's the point? I'm headed vaguely toward the "taxi" which is supposedly the quickest way back to my hostel.

Suddenly, I get the sense I am traveling back to some distant age. All the modern chaos of Bangkok quickly fades away and I find myself in an eighteenth-century fishing village. The wood huts, lack of automobiles, and rough-hewn cobblestone paths disorient me, but I know it's still today because of that rain. This is the hardest rain I've ever felt, and it goes on like this for nearly two hours.

Now I'm crossing a rickety by-way leading to an old wooden dock. The "taxi" is a boat which will take me back through the center of the city to a metro station.

Were this truly the eighteenth century, I would probably take a boat all the way home. Its once extensive system of canals earned Bangkok recognition as the "Venice of the East."

Beauty and nostalgia long since gave way to industry and practicality. This dirty river and its informal water taxis are just about all that remain of a forgotten era.

Nonetheless, this dock and this whole scene are as real as it gets. As I stand under the leaky shelter of the dock's straw roof, I can't help but feel like a true explorer.

I am on the other side of the world in a small, random, but pure moment of authentic wonder and discovery. I briefly picture myself as Indiana Jones or someone on a fearless hunt for some lost treasure or artifact, something really inspiring, of course.

The moment quickly fades as the water taxi comes and whisks me back into civilization. As I watch the dock drift into the distance, I once again enter reality as just another of the millions of tourists to Bangkok's sights and sounds.

The rain stops somewhere along the way, and I glance down the river one last time. Through the rising mist and steam and putrid smog shoots a vivid rainbow, soaring majestically above the dock and into the clouds. I wonder for a moment how all these other people got here, what they are doing here, and if they've ever seen something so beautiful in this city of 8 million.

* * *

A few days later, I peer lazily out the train window at the blurred, passing Thai jungle, still unable to shake the feeling which hasn't left me since touch down. I am vividly aware that I am almost directly half-way around the world from home, starting from scratch, again.

This was another one of those moments like that day with the grass in my toes, when my parents dropped me off at college, where I thought I was hitting the reset button on life.

This time though – as I embraced again this moment as a floating, disconnected individual – I wasn't searching for a new me or a new identity, not explicitly anyway. This time, with the jungle and the pulsating, dripping heat, and the rice paddies and their workers whizzing by at 80 mph, I was seeking a purpose.

To be fair, I wasn't quite starting from scratch either. Along with the myriad advantages afforded to people from the "pinnacle" out on our personal quests for whatever end, the privilege of elite connection was very much still along for the ride. Jeremy's friend Matt – the Harvard Law School guy — is waiting for me and we take a tuk-tuk back to his apartment. Matt welcomes me to town and helps me get established.

* * *

Two weeks later, I find myself staring dumbfounded into a dark, musty 5x8 closet. This closet is my first job out of college. This job is a jumbled, leaning, messy tower of papers stacked floor to ceiling. Each of these papers tells a story of the journey it's been on, crumpled and torn, smudged with dirt and occasionally smeared with something that looks like blood. Beyond the surface, I find these stories – like Bangkok's billboards – totally indecipherable, merely symbols on a page, symbols from the languages of Thai, Karen, Shan, Burmese.

In my first six months, I was tasked with the creation of a searchable database from FBR's thousands of human rights reports. These reports contained sensitive and important information about the who, what, when and where of atrocities committed by the Burmese military against villagers across the vast north of the country. Given FBR's clandestine access to the war-torn regions of the country during a period when access was closed, this leaning, musty stack of papers was a potential gold mine for international criminal prosecutors.

My job was to build a network of translators and then manage all the data entry for key information from the reports into a dynamic database. It was grueling work.

Yet as I went about this humble task, I could not help but learn. As I recruited translators, I learned about their stories escaping a brutal civil war and their concern for family members still on the other side.

As I proofread translated reports, I learned about the horrific atrocities inside Myanmar about which the rest of the world could only speculate, and largely chose to ignore.

As I built the database and managed the data entry, I learned about the reporting process and the data itself and about what legal advocates like Matt needed to make such things useful.

As I learned, I became expert-enough in some of this to play a hand in strengthening FBR's data collection, analysis, and reporting processes. Months later, this learning positioned me to help lead trainings for FBR's local teams around Northern Myanmar.

For years after that, this tedious initial work instilled in me a deep appreciation for the importance of (and challenges inherent to) strong data collection, management, and analysis in humanitarian/development crisis management.

More than a decade of learning experiences later, I still draw on the visceral lessons of this initial task as I lead teams and advise government leaders on how to make effective decisions on the basis of data, evidence, and information collected in less than ideal circumstances.

I think it is always like this with humble tasks. Deep knowledge, useful skills, creative solutions, and the ability to lead well always seem to rise from exposure to the thankless tasks, the job done from its ugly beginning. For a life spent resisting, even running from such experiences, this 5x8 closet was a formative moment.

* * *

Figuring out how to bring order out of information chaos wasn't the only challenge in store for me during those months.

Before I could get clearance to attend the reporting trainings, I had to pass a series of physical and tactical tests. Getting to the trainings behind closed borders in Shan, Karen, and Kachin States required strenuous multi-day hikes, and we weren't coming in empty-handed.

Everyone carried a "full" minimum 45lb pack of malaria meds, bed nets, rice, medical supplies, and whatever else was needed.

I was in decent shape, but trekking through sweltering heat in a mountainous, mine-filled war zone with ex-Special Ops-types was a whole new level.

Throughout my indoctrination into FBR's world, I was certainly still aiming to prove something vague and unattainable to myself. But this time, I also had a deeper motivation. I was humbled by the gravity of the work I was preparing for and became dedicated – if only for a short time – to ensuring I was ready to be more of a help than a burden in a land which would push me to my limits.

Alongside learning the skills and pushing my body, I was also trying desperately to learn the basics about what the heck was going on in Myanmar. I continued to learn about the context from reading whatever I could get my hands on, from watching documentaries, from asking millions of questions to the folks in my office, and by traveling around with Matt.

Matt was kind enough to let me tag along on his fact-finding missions about the crisis on the other side of the border.

It was on these trips where I heard firsthand stories about lives destroyed by war, specific tales of human suffering caused by a more universal story of human brokenness.

It was on these trips when I began to question our own role as Americans in this ongoing suffering: how much we had done, how little we were doing.

It was on these trips when I began to catch a glimpse of the beauty and wonder and hope arising from solidarity with the world's poor and marginalized as I considered a path I might follow.

Chapter 25

The great tragedy in the Church is not that rich Christians do not care about the poor but that rich Christians do not know the poor... I truly believe that when the rich meet the poor, riches will have no meaning. And when the rich meet the poor, we will see poverty come to an end.

Shane Claiborne, The Irresistible Revolution: Living as an Ordinary Radical

Some adventures fall suddenly into your lap – like a chance encounter with an inspiring future employer.

Other adventures are thrust upon you with a vengeance, rocking you from a comfort zone – like a hard push up a sweltering jungled mountain trail with a heavy pack.

Others still weave their way into your life with a subtle breeze which requires a discerning heart to fully grasp. These are the adventures which take a lifetime to develop.

My adventure with Compassion International started 25 years ago in Fairfax, VA, with a Haitian boy named Santis. I've never actually met Santis, though I've known him since we were very young. My parents were introduced to Compassion's work somewhere in the deep recesses of my latent early memories. Eventually they decided it would be a good family activity to sponsor a child.

Letters from Santis were the first cracked windows to a world outside my bubble of American prosperity. Though it would take a long time for those windows to open more fully, it was through these openings that his life – and the lives of billions of others – first touched my own.

Years later, my internship at Compassion forced me the rest of the way through this small window to the world now wide open before me.

The internship also provided connections to some cool folks at Compassion's Thailand Field Office. At one point, another window opened when these new friends asked me to visit a project and write a story for their donor newsletter.

* * *

The paved road and rental car got me to a small town within 24 miles of the project. We were still in the pre-smart phone era, so I wrote down the directions on a scrap of paper, hopped on a borrowed bicycle, and rode off into the jungle.

Two hours (and a few bike chain-related mishaps) later, I pulled up to the project. Huay Keaw Kuhn is a tiny Karen village less than a mile from the Burmese border.

Much of Thailand's most extreme poverty is concentrated in this region where hundreds of thousands of Burmese refugees survive on next to nothing.

Years ago, the residents of Huay Keaw Kuhn were forced from their homes when a village with the same name just across the river was destroyed by the Burmese army. It was at this moment that Compassion reached into their lives and extended an unfamiliar taste of hope to their children.

My brief time at the project was pure joy. The teachers and Compassion staff graciously showed me around and gave me more than I needed for my short story.

"Maybe you come back for good and live with us and teach English I think," said one of the teachers. The half-joking thought turned into a discussion which turned into an offer of sorts.

In another life, I might have done it. I still question how much help I would've been. Nonetheless, I count this and other gestures welcoming me into such rich communities as deeply compelling.

Compelling, not because I necessarily see a white, American

guy teaching English to Burmese children from a grass hut on the Thai border as some sort of elevated calling. In fact, there is so much wrong with this image theoretically and pragmatically it gives me cold sweats.

Alluring, not because – all these years later – I necessarily see Compassion's model (or any programmatic model for that matter) as the end-all-be-all of poverty alleviation work. I certainly do not.

Rather, I count this offer and others like it as particularly inspiring because I've come to recognize the revolutionary potential of deep relationship between the rich and the poor. For, when relationships are deep enough and authentic enough and close enough, solidarity cannot help but form between these two divergent worlds.

To be clear, solidarity is not slum-tourism or white saviorism or "development" or even charity in the traditional sense. Rather, solidarity is that moment when we realize that despite our differences and the uncrossable chasms of our divergent worlds, we have something undeniably in common with our fellow human. It is in such moments that true generosity is born – that deeper, almost irrational generosity in which control is released, power is given up for the good of another. In such moments, there is something vital and lasting, something truly radical and perhaps even transcendent.

* * *

Years later, as a practitioner in the strange industry working toward the contested ideas of "development" and "global justice," I sometimes lose sight of this core truth about solidarity.

Today, we know the causes of poverty: ubiquitous historical and contemporary oppression and exploitation; unequal provision of key goods like quality healthcare, education, social protection, and infrastructure; and a global economic system which ensures that some people are born at or have the ability to reach the "pinnacle" regardless of their merit, while others do not.

These are systemic problems to which we can and should envision, test, and scale programmatic and political solutions. Done well, these are worthy pursuits, and I'm honored to contribute in very small ways to such big, uncertain projects.

Yet on a far deeper plane of reality, these are all human problems rooted in universal selfishness, greed, and fear.

As we in the western do-gooder industrial complex concoct "solutions" to these "problems," we often fail to remember that we are not all-knowing. We do not and cannot approach complex issues like poverty, inequality, or violence from a balanced, unbiased perspective. We cannot achieve absolute or even reasonable levels of objectivity or rationality and our delusion that we can is only making matters worse.

Neither we nor our ideas nor our western framing nor our techniques or programs are powerful enough to "systematically" fix the root causes of poverty and oppression in this world – problems inescapably linked and perpetuated by our very nature.

When we rest our hope on systems and programs – themselves built by broken humans with complex, imperfect, often contradictory motives and limited perspective – we miss the point and we miss our call.

* * *

As a Christian, I am forever bound up in the story of Jesus and its implications for our wander-lost lives. The radical narrative of his life on this earth is, to me, the living breathing "good news" – the answer, if you will, to all these damning questions about the separation between rich and poor.

Jesus willingly took on material poverty and eventually

marginalization to state violence in order to demonstrate a radical solidarity with the vulnerable and the broken. Over and over in the Bible, He asks us to do the same.

The Sermon on the Mount was not delivered as a proposal to program poverty away or maintain arbitrary distance between it and Himself. Rather, it was and is a revolutionary call to share love and solidarity with others who suffer its scourge.

Yet, distances and barriers between lives like mine and those in the village of Huay Keaw Kuhn are enormous.

They are comfortably maintained by those powerful, unjust, not-quite invisible systems with which we are all complicit. And we can't "plan" these injustices out of existence. Our carefully laid programs and strategies are never quite bold enough to abandon the towering "pinnacle" from which they are formed.

As such, a commitment to solidarity asserts itself as more central than our aspirations for measurable "progress." In a massive, impersonal world, it is far too easy to lose track of the windows to our common humanity amidst all that space between us and them.

* * *

In the fading light, I rode back to town through that winding jungle path – pondering these lessons not fully formed and the windows which continued to open before me.

I didn't quite know what to make of my mounting devastation at the gravity of the world's plight. Yet I found myself utterly captivated by the consistent rising of the universe to meet this naive, stumbling traveler from the "pinnacle."

Chapter 26

In a car you're always in a compartment, and because you're used to it you don't realize that through that car window everything you see is just more TV. You're a passive observer and it is all moving by you boringly in a frame. On a motorcycle the frame is gone. You're completely in contact with it all. You're in the scene, not just watching it anymore, and the sense of presence is overwhelming.

Robert M. Pirsig, Zen and the Art of Motorcycle Maintenance: An Inquiry Into Values

My season in Southeast Asia was marked by periodic windows of time out on the road, away from my primary intended purpose at FBR. Some of those windows – like this border bicycle ride – were more "important." Not important because I *did* anything of lasting value, but important because they represented an explicit grappling with the big questions of global injustice and my role in it.

Other windows were more, shall we say, "frivolous fun." At this stage, I often failed to differentiate between the deeper transformations and those fleeting moments of personal satisfaction which emanate from the impetuous excess of free-spirited travel.

These trips, particularly the frivolous fun ones, the ones divorced of any pretense of larger purpose, continued to reveal to me the beauty of travel – and also its limitations.

I found travel to be a medicine for my restless soul, if not necessarily a cure. To be totally honest, the rush of disconnected jaunts – surrendering to the mercy of whatever experience lies around that next curve of the road – hit me like a strong narcotic.

* * *

A few days before Christmas, my inbox held an early gift: official acceptance to my first-choice grad program where I would enroll to study International Development and Economic History the following academic year.

Given my unremarkable undergraduate grades, I had no business even applying to this school. I recognized the grace extended me here and wanted to celebrate. Problem was, the FBR office had just closed for a few weeks and most of my friends were back in the states for the holidays.

In this moment of restless exuberance and momentary isolation and probably a touch of anxiety at the possibilities of the future, I pined after some of that calming, metaphysical medicine of spontaneous travel – where everything is new and anything can happen and nothing else matters but the fleeting, ephemeral *now*.

With no other rationale and no further planning, I decided that a (slightly early) visa renewal run to Vientiane, Laos, was as good a celebratory trip as any.

The next morning, I loaded a bag with my laptop, a change of clothes, and a few snacks into my motorcycle's panniers and took off on a ride east.

I figured I'd make a weekend out of the outbound trip and take another two days back. Within a few hours, the beautiful winding northern Thai roads lulled me into an unsuspecting rhythm. 7 hours and 400 miles later, I rolled into Vientiane on the Thai/Laotian border.

As I rode into town, I stopped at a hostel and bought a night. It was the first time in my life I'd ever not known where I'd stay that evening. Reveling in the adrenaline rush of the ride and the release of control offered by this new plane of spontaneity soothed and awakened something in me.

Books and books have been written on the magic that happens traveling on a motorcycle through strange lands with no real plan. I will not attempt to duplicate that here. I will only say this magic certainly worked on me.

That evening, I lingered around the common table with the other lost and wandering souls as we swapped stories from our individual journeys on a somewhat common path. Amidst such rarefied company, I realized that, with the office closed, I had three weeks to kill and no real plans back in my home away from home. As I sat there with my friends for the night, I made the decision not to return to Chiang Mai the next day, but instead to head east as far as the road would take me.

For several days I rolled through the soft, southern Laotian countryside, stopping in villages when I grew weary and asking around for places to eat and stay.

I can't quite say for sure what route I took, only that it was beautiful. I passed through numerous national parks and bio-reserves and ultimately another colonial legacy: the international border between Laos and Vietnam bureaucratically separating a hinterland once not so formally divided.

A few days later, the South China Sea finally opened up before me somewhere near Thanh Hoa in central Vietnam. I gave the North/South decision about a minute of thought before cranking the accelerator, dropping the clutch, and drifting the tires right.

Looking back, North was probably the better option – famed Halong Bay was no more than 100 miles "left" of where I hit the ocean.

South was great too, though. I count the three days meandering through Vietnamese fishing villages and along the quiet country roads amongst the most tranquil in my life.

On day 10, I looked at a map for the first time and pieced together the route I'd traversed. I made the "responsible" decision and turned the bike right again, heading west.

* * *

I say "responsible" because life for a traveler in Southeast Asia always seemed biased toward the inverse. Though my life was full, the beck and call of a lifetime of Saturdays was ever-present.

When I first arrived at my home base of Chiang Mai, I'd taken two weeks to adjust before starting my job at FBR. Yet it took me exactly one day to find an apartment and realize that a life of leisure wasn't something I'd need to wait for retirement at 65 to achieve.

Again, the privilege of my English-language ability and strong connections smoothed my entry to a new life. Within three days, I'd lined up two consistent freelance writing gigs which would require about three days a month of work and – with monthly expenses below $1,000 – could support a comfortable life here indefinitely.

During those first weeks, I would run early in the morning, take Thai lessons till noon, grab some incredibly cheap, delicious food for lunch, write a bit, and then play pick-up basketball and ultimate frisbee until dark. Usually I'd shower, then head to one of several dozen amazing bars to play pool and listen to stories from locals and fellow travelers – or jazz music from the best guitarist I'd ever seen perform live.

It was during those first weeks that I bought the used 249cc Honda dual sport which propelled me on my spontaneous cross-continental overland journey, amongst other adventures. The feeling of freedom and conquest with the wind in my face as I flew up steep mountains and through exotic jungles and quaint villages both awakened and intoxicated me like nothing I'd ever experienced.

Were it not for the constant reminder of a deeper reality offered by my job and the questions which had begun to swirl, I might never have awakened from this "Hotel California" dream.

* * *

After another blissful, entranced week guiding my bike vaguely in the direction of home, I crossed into Cambodia. The whole trip, I'd been warned that this would be the dangerous country with its relative lawlessness, endemic corruption, and propensity to state violence. Perhaps I was just lucky but I found my time in the Kingdom of Wonder as tranquil and welcoming as the others.

Riding out from the hot, humid capital city of Phnom Penh, I would pass unaware a faded yellow French colonial building just off the main drag. This building would one day – over a decade later – serve as my home, the desk from which I'd pen these very words.

The next day, I passed back into Thailand, bumbling my way into the low-key beach town of Nang Ram, a bit south of Pattaya. I lazed a few days floating in the bay and hired an old fisherman to take me out to gorgeous Samae San island one afternoon.

At this point, I began to have some difficulty imagining the 18-some-hour ride back to Chiang Mai. So, on day 20 of the most spontaneous three weeks of my young life, I rode the 2.5 hours to a train station north of Bangkok and tapped out. For $80 (about a week's worth of expenses on that trip), I got the bike loaded onto a train and procured a private cabin to sleep the rest of the way to Chiang Mai.

On that train ride back, I was the king of the world and I slept like a baby. Though I hadn't done anything of quantifiable value, I had broken through a plane en route to travel nirvana and felt at one with the open road.

To phrase things like a true addict: in that moment, this feeling, this certain type of "freedom," was all that mattered.

The bigger consequences of such choices – this mindset multiplied across a lifetime and across a generation of would-be wanderlost travelers like me – would not sink in for quite some time.

Chapter 27

A neighbor is not he whom I find in my path, but rather he in whose path I place myself, he whom I approach and actively seek.
Gustavo Gutiérrez, A Theology of Liberation

A few months later another window for some carefree travel arose, and I jumped at the opportunity. My dad was headed to Australia for a business trip. We thought it a grand idea for me to meet him there and spend the next week hiking through Tasmania.

I flew in via Malaysia to Brisbane, Australia, not because that's where my dad was, but because flights were cheaper to Brisbane than to New Castle (some 500 miles down the coast). I'd purchased a connecting bus ticket for the next day at noon, but I now faced 24 hours to kill.

I also faced a serious problem for those 24 hours: cash flow. I'd canceled my credit card the week prior due to fraudulent activity. Capital One mailed a new one to my folks' house, and I'd get it the following day from my dad. That didn't help me this day though.

This would've been fine if my debit card had worked.

It didn't.

Fraud alert flagged that I'd once again shifted continents and the small Colorado Credit Union was closed until Monday.

My remaining Thai baht converted to about 20 Australian Dollars. That would have to suffice until I reconnected with my credit card down the coast.

A reasonable human being would've taken this as a sign to lay low in the airport for a day, buying cheap, high calorie foods and drinking from the water fountain to stretch the funds.

However, the impetuous, shoestring nature of my motorcycle ride a few months earlier had quickly melded into my identity as a traveler, and I was eager for a repeat performance.

Upon clearing customs, I started seeing signs for the QuickSilver World Surfing Championships which were, coincidentally, going on that very day in nearby Gold Coast.

My luck was turning. There was a free event, and it was only 14 miles away.

I got out to the highway and started walking.

Within about a mile out in the Aussie sun, all my childhood warnings about hitchhiking went out the window, and the thumb went up. Five minutes later a semi pulled over and I hopped in.

Another travel plane crossed. Another dose of that potent drug taken.

Only later would I read about the terrifying number of hitchhikers murdered by a serial killing long-distance trucker along that exact Australian highway just months before.

Thankfully I was not to become one of them, and ten minutes later I hopped out with all limbs intact, right in front of the Surf Tournament.

This was the first time I'd ever seen a barrel wave big enough to surf through or a surfer good enough to do so and make it look easy. The novelty was totally enthralling.

* * *

An hour later and I am starving. It's 2pm and I haven't eaten anything... and there's also that problem of money. Walking the Gold Coast boardwalk is depressing when you're broke. Everything is so expensive and the food on people's plates doesn't look especially filling. It's a pretty upscale place.

Then, I stumble upon it. "All you can eat pancakes!! $11.99!!"

Without hesitation, I enter. As I am being seated, I notice a board with a big Australian dude's picture and the number 26. It was the record for most pancakes consumed.

I'm not a big person, but I can put down food like I am. Why not go for it, I think.

She brings the first three decent sized pancakes. I annihilate them.

Impressed at the speed, she brings three more. Gone.

As she goes back for round three, I realize my approach is all wrong. If I stuff myself now, I will be absolutely starving in 3–4 hours. I need to play this strategically instead of competitively.

When she delivers 7, 8, and 9, I smoothly pull two off the table and into my open backpack, then eat the third.

Same with 10–12.

Same with 13–15.

Same with 16–18.

When she brings out 19–21, a group starts to form and I am compelled to eat all three. The gig is up. Eight pancakes should be more than sufficient to get me through the next 20 or so hours. I am happy.

A larger crowd forms to watch me eat 22–24.

Then, decision time. The final plate. I have eaten 16 pancakes at this point and am pretty full, but 3 more aren't going to make me puke.

Twenty-six was the record, though. While I feel no conscience pangs about the 1600 or so calories of stolen carbs in my bag, it also doesn't feel quite right. I may be a thief, but I ain't a cheat.

I slowly eat about a third of the plate, feign nausea and throw down my fork, calling it quits.

Encouragements and cheers and some goading erupt from the small crowd, but I am firm. I will not be their hero today. I will not sit on that throne of lies.

I pay my $11.99 and walk back to the surf contest feeling pretty good about my "interesting" moral compass.

When the competition wraps up and the sun begins to dip, I go for a walk again through the boardwalk. Before I realize it, darkness has fallen.

I find I'm not quite bold enough to hitchhike at night, so I decide to sleep out on the beach.

I lay my pack down and look up at the stars. As I take in this moment, I begin to think about how I've gotten to this point of temporary homelessness and how this wouldn't be so much fun if I had to do it more frequently.

Just then, up walks a guy who looks like he might not have a choice in the matter.

"Any money, sir?"

I want to say, "Look at me, dude. Do you think I have any money?"

Instead, I say, "Unfortunately not, you?"

He says no.

I ask what he's up to and he seems like a nice guy. Apparently, he's from Perth and hitchhiked across the country. Something rough happened in his past, but I decide not to pry.

I'm feeling a bit peckish and pull out a pancake. His eyes perk up and I ask if he's hungry.

"Starving, man."

I pull out another pancake and toss it to him.

Over the next hour, we share my pancakes and his box of wine. I recount the story of my little adventure, and we talk about the ethics of need in the world. I confess I'm not so much poor as stupid. He says being poor makes him do things that feel stupid sometimes.

As I sip his cheap wine, I learn a bit about the welfare system in Australia upon which he now depends. As he eats my hotcakes, he also gets my hot takes on the conflict in Myanmar though I still know very little.

Being in his presence somehow makes my little jaunt feel self-indulgent. But then again, in his presence, in a rare glimpse of authentic contact with someone who's had it rough, this whole little jaunt almost feels valuable.

Sometime well after midnight, I drift off.

It's 3:45am, still dark when I'm awakened by radio feedback and shining lights.

"Up! Get up, you vagrants!"

We shuffle up, disoriented.

"I've told you enough times, this time I'm booking you."

I look at my new friend, but they are looking at me. Mistaken identity, I guess.

The two Aussie-cops handcuff us and put us in the back of their car. I'm a bit nervous, but I can't really figure out what I was doing wrong. There weren't any signs saying we couldn't sleep here. My friend doesn't look overly concerned either. I play it cool.

Fifteen minutes later we arrive back at the station. I show my license and passport, and it is very clear that I'm a harmless American tourist. It looks like I'm going to be released.

"What will happen to him?" I ask.

"What's it to you?" They say.

"Well, that's my friend."

"What's his name?"

I stumble. Honestly, I never asked his name. He knew mine, but I hadn't ever asked. I don't know why I didn't, but I feel terrible.

In the end, they decide to let us both go with a warning: no more sleeping on the beach.

It's around 9:30am by the time we're free men again, and I need to get back to Brisbane for my bus. My new friend says he should probably leave town now to avoid another unpleasant encounter. He'll head down the coast and camp-out there.

We hail a semi-truck and hop aboard.

Not too many more words pass between us. I feel as though I've betrayed him, as though I betrayed a rare moment to truly connect with another human.

Sure, we shared a moment, but mostly, I spent it, as I so often do, absorbed in my own story, failing to truly be changed by the complexities of another. Worse yet, I thought we had made a connection and only later realized I didn't even know his name.

As I prepare to hop out, I leave him with the rest of my money, $5 and change, plus the last three pancakes.

He says thanks, smiles, and genuinely doesn't look hurt. Even so, I kick myself.

His name was Tim.

Chapter 28

If discontent is your disease, travel is your medicine.
Jedidiah Jenkins, To Shake the Sleeping Self

Two days into the trip, my dad injures his shoulder while sand boarding. We spend the next week in the hospital instead of backpacking Tasmania. It still ends up being a great time together.

At the end of our trip to Australia, I say goodbye and board the flight for my first leg back to Kuala Lumpur. I'm flying a Boeing 777 on Malaysia Airlines, the same plane which, just three years later, would disappear over the Indian Ocean en route to Beijing with 227 passengers and 12 staff onboard.

This flight arrives safely, but just barely.

As of early 2022, I've logged over 700,000 air miles to nearly 80 countries and have never encountered turbulence like this.

Lights are flashing on and off. People are screaming. Air masks come down several times. I am fairly convinced we are going to die at numerous points during the voyage.

Fearful, immature faith recommitments and quickly forgotten promises to God ensue.

We arrive at Kuala Lumpur International Airport at 9:00am, and my next flight doesn't leave until 6:00am the following day. I'm totally exhausted, having already been awake 21 hours. I am still, however, actively seeking my next travel-induced metaphysical high.

This morning, my regular *jonesing* is compounded by an intense, immediate desire to squeeze every inch out of life. Such compulsions tend to be the more powerful "spiritual" ramifications to emerge from perceived near-death experiences like the one on my inbound flight.

With increased motivation in hand, I decide to venture into

Kuala Lumpur.

KLIA is about 40 miles from downtown. There's a bus that takes you into the city for about $6. I buy a return.

Not wanting to carry my luggage with me – and, clearly, having learned exactly nothing about the importance of spare cash from my recent Australian adventure – I check everything except my ticket, passport, and $20 in local currency onto my next flight.

I board the bus around noon. When I de-board an hour later, I'm given a schedule for the return trips: every hour on the hour until 10:00pm. Should be plenty of time to explore, return, and take a nap in the terminal.

Wandering around, I'm struck by KL. The Petronas Towers, the world's largest twin buildings, are a magnificent wall of glass before me, true temples of opulence. I'm drawn to the spectacle and walk up to them, now less than 300 feet in front of me and over 1,500 feet high.

Turning 180 degrees, I see a slum. Malaysia is the most unequal country on the planet and the visceral reality of the difference is on full display here at its economic epicenter.

I grab a late lunch nearby for a few dollars. I sit there, pondering what to do with my privileged sadness at such staggering inequality. Turning around again, I see a luxury fitness center which looks directly out at the towers, this makeshift slum in its shadow.

I realize I haven't worked out in a few days. Perhaps a jog while taking in this scene a bit more deeply will help.

I go upstairs and pretend to be an expat moving to the area in order to get a free "trial" day pass. This has become a regular schtick when I need a workout in a new city. I like to think of it as a heroic moment of sorts; taking a little something from the wealthy and hanging out where I don't belong make me feel like I'm beating the system somehow.

Today, I see such rebellions as misguided, but in the moment, I thought my cause noble and my motives pure.

I hop on the treadmill and look out over the city. The sunset behind the towers is stunning, almost inspiring. I notice the slum again and instinctively turn away, the hypocrisy of my selfish rebellion still failing to sink in.

Looking back, I now see these small rebellions as unenlightened uses of my privilege. While it is true that in such acts I take something from higher social strata, I am only able to do so because of my skin color, my native tongue, and the confidence I'm able to present in such situations – all stemming from a life at the "pinnacle."

Further, economically speaking, this behavior amounts to little more than rent-seeking, and in our society the costs of those rents are more efficiently transferred to those lowest on the value-chain than those at the top. In short, the selfish rebellion is ignorant and counter-productive. I'm no Robin Hood.

I change it up and head over to the weights and then finally to the stationary bike.

It is 9:30pm before I'm sauna-ed, showered, and out the door. I walk the 15 minutes back to the station and see a bus taking off.

Still a bit early, I'm unconcerned. I wander up to the station, sit down and wait.

And wait.

And wait.

At around 10:20, I ask someone.

"The last bus always leaves from here 15 minutes before 10."

This makes no sense. My schedule says 10!!

I ask two other people and get the same answer. The last light rail (which goes 80% of the way to the airport) has also departed.

Panic sets in.

I have $9.30 cents left, a US passport, and half a bottle of Gatorade. My flight takes off in 7.5 hours 40 miles from here and I've now been awake for over 33 hours – exercising the last 2 hours plus.

I hail a cab. $30 he says. No way.

I hail another. $28. I haggle a bit and get to $25 but then have to tell him to leave as well.

Now, I walk over to the group of taxi drivers, and ask them how far someone is willing to take me for $9.30.

Even in my desperation and with a group of competitors, the best answer I get is "the E6/AH2 intersection." AH2 is the road which runs into the airport. The intersection is 15 miles from the terminal. I have no other options and hop in.

At 11:30, we pull up to the intersection and my driver slows to a stop.

"From here, just walk straight. Don't turn."

I have nothing left to offer the driver. I can't give him my passport. I need the 16 ounces of Gatorade to face a long hike in the humid Malaysian heat, still well above 80° F in the middle of the night. He doesn't want my shoes or shirt. Believe me, I offer.

The sign on the side of the road says, "KLIA 25km" (15.5 miles). I start walking.

This is about the most physically exhausted I've ever felt, but the initial panic has long-since subsided. I somehow find myself elated at the adventurous hits which just keep coming.

* * *

The "medicine" I was taking with mounting frequency via memorable, miserable, self-inflicted little jaunts like this one in Malaysia was curing me – and it wasn't.

This string of spontaneous adventures was progressively healing me from a lifetime in the bubble of secure American affluence as it forced me to wrestle with the big unanswered questions and the contingent nature of reality. The wrestling was beginning to transform the direction of my life.

Yet the irony does not escape me. This self-medication was developing a frantic, desperate, selfish pattern of increasingly reckless experiences: a growing need to put myself in such situations in order to feel whole.

* * *

According to my watch, it's 1:30am when I pass another sign which reads, "KLIA 15km" (9.3 miles).

I'm long past my reservations about night-time hitch-hiking, but not a single other person or car is out on the road. I think I see things moving back and forth across the highway, but I'm not sure. I'm too tired to be scared.

It's 4:00am when I see the 5km sign (3.1 miles). My Gatorade bottle is now empty.

Thirty-nine hours without sleep and my brain is complete mush. It takes me the better part of 10 minutes to calculate my pace and realize I'm cutting it way too close.

I start to run. Granted, it's not much of a run, but I'm moving faster now and my blood and brain are responding to the shift. It's still pitch-black outside and I still see the phantoms jumping across the road. Not people or animals or anything discernible, just amorphous shapes. I begin to question if I'm hallucinating.

Just then, I notice the lights of the airport. I hope I'm not hallucinating.

At 4:40am, I arrive at the airport, utterly exhausted, dehydrated, and delusional. I'm also now, strangely – pathologically even – totally in my element.

No time or money for a drink though. In the zone, I sprint for security.

Much of the night was a blur, but I'll never forget *that* moment. I put my passport on the conveyer belt and begin to walk through the scanner. Just then, I hear Sgt. Pepper's Lonely Hearts Club Band playing over the airport speakers. I look up as I walk through security and see, I kid you not, I *see* the music coming from the speakers. Not the words, the music itself. I can't describe it in any other way, but it was beautiful and disorienting.

This "medicine," the ragged edges of this thing which was meant to release and free and cure me is starting to reveal some unpleasant side effects.

I shake my head hard, grab my passport, walk up to a water fountain, and submerge for a socially inappropriate length of time.

It is now 5:20am, more than 41 miserable, sweating, hallucinating, striving, self-medicating hours since my eyes and body and soul last rested.

I crawl into the belly of the plane – this contraption which almost killed me a day earlier – and fall into a deep and dreamless sleep.

Chapter 29

We commit ourselves to the journey toward reconciliation because
we believe it is right even when we are not sure how it will progress
or end. We believe that walking down the path to peace offers a way
better than violence and an instrument more powerful than force
to conduct the affairs of humankind. We pray that others will join
us.

John Paul Lederach, The Journey Toward Reconciliation

A wise friend once told me, "I often find I don't know why I do
what I do; what I really believe; or even who I really am until I
write."

In the midst of these journeys on the other side of the world,
I found the same was true for myself.

* * *

Back in Chiang Mai, there was much to process as I prepared
for an extended trip – not in further search of self – but into the
war-torn jungles of Northern Myanmar with FBR.

This learning journey was deeply formed through my
exposure to missionaries and aid workers and diplomats and
backpackers and pastors and professors. Their perspectives lent
credibility to my growing belief that all is not so simple as it
seems looking for oneself out on the open road.

Daily interactions and conversations with Thai people from
a broad spectrum of society added to the happy confusion.

I was by no means an expert on war and violent conflict,
but I was learning quickly. The sheer complexity of this single
situation in Myanmar – the parties involved, the actors at fault,
the myriad attempted solutions and how they had failed – was
casting irrefutable shadows of gray on the fantasy of a black

and white world I'd once embraced as real.

Amidst these shadows, I continued to wrestle more deeply with the oppression I saw around me.

Amidst these shadows, I continued, albeit gradually, to gain awareness of the depravity I encountered within myself.

Amidst these shadows, I began to honestly grapple with the truly difficult questions, the ones I was always afraid to ask.

As is wont to happen, all that thinking, and wrestling, and talking, and listening and learning began to form in me a new way of looking at the world. I longed for a way to solidify all I was learning, to make some sort of sense of it all, even if that sense was that there is no sense.

And so it was that I began to write and learn who I was and what I believed.

* * *

From the beginning of all this learning, my writing focused on topics of culture, politics, and the world beyond our borders. This is the concrete subject matter of my interests, my observations, even my profession.

Yet I tend to find myself drawn by a consistent final question when sifting through such matters. *What does this mean for the Church? What does this mean for a people formed by the particular story of Christ's good news to the world?*

* * *

As I continued to wrestle and write and in turn learn and believe things, I became convinced of a core truth about this messy, fragmented world.

As Stanley Hauerwas frequently states in his unique way, "the world desperately needs the Church to show it what it is not."

The world doesn't need the followers of Christ to show it a journey toward dogmatism or a clinging to security or a propensity to violence.

The world knows those paths well. Rather, the Church – if it is to be of any use to itself or the world – must demonstrate the value of its particularity, its specific history and purpose.

In a world gone mad for the universal, the Church must re-become a culture grounded in the unique, specific story of Christ. In this story, we reject our late-modern, hyper-materialist aspirations and state violence-drenched security. In this story, we accept our own marginalization, persecution, even martyrdom as the sole earthly birthright for following a Christ crucified for the world.

If we can arrive at a renewed, honest focus on this truer story and excitement for this deeper journey, our Church just might be able to offer the world a path to the hope it so desperately needs.

And through this story, this journey, this path, we might just stumble into a culture we can call our own.

* * *

Deep in the midst of the world's longest running conflicts, Dave Eubank is working to build such a culture.

Dave is a humble guy who probably would object to my saying so, but he is easily the most courageous and inspiring human I've ever met. More importantly, the directionality of his courage seems laser-aligned with the story Christ asks his people to re-tell in their days on this earth.

For nearly three decades, Dave, a former US Army Ranger and Special Forces Officer has built and led a subversive yet peaceful liberation movement bringing hope and unity to the divided ethnic groups of northern Myanmar (and later, Syria and Iraq) through an offering of selfless, unconditional love.

Practically speaking, his organization provides training and equipment for relief teams. These teams, led by indigenous people, pursue humanitarian missions throughout the war-torn regions of their own countries.

Since 1954, Myanmar has been dominated by a military junta which, among other atrocities, pursued a campaign of brutality against the country's 150-plus distinct ethnic minorities. For much of this time, in an attempt to conceal the nature of their atrocities, the government closed a vast majority of the country to foreigners, including humanitarian aid and relief organizations. Thus, all assistance given by FBR and the tiny number of other organizations working inside had to be done under the radar with local support.

From a geo-political strategy perspective, sneaking across borders and lending aid to underdog rebel groups outside formal mechanisms is generally frowned upon, as it can lengthen the conflict or compete with other strategic goals of the international community.

Yet from the perspective of a Church called to help the most vulnerable, what other options do we have? As we wait for our theories to play out as expected (or not) and our governments to act on our behalf (or not), who else is serving these unarmed villagers under attack?

FBR, unlike any other "relief group" I've ever encountered, displays an unwavering commitment to stand with the people they serve. In fact, this is the first lesson taught to Rangers in training. If the villagers are in danger, FBR team members must not abandon them even if it means sacrificing their own life.

This is not just grandiose language. It happens. I count as one of my life's greatest privileges to have known some of these "rangers" who died because of their willingness to stand with the vulnerable.

Beyond the specific martyrs, this ethos filters down to the very core of work that sneaks across hostile borders and through

rough country to show solidarity with the teams and villagers. A willingness to serve in spite of the continuous physical risks has built an immense amount of local trust over the years.

It is a commitment that starts with the founder who brings his young family deep into active war zones for months at a time. You might question the wisdom and ethics of such a decision.

For Dave and his courageous wife, Karen, it came down to a simple question: *How are our kids any different from the kids on the other side of the border?*

Chatting with Dave one evening on a hillside in rebel-controlled Shan State, he said something I won't ever forget.

"Yes, we might die. But, if we do, it won't be for a cause. It won't be for a revolution. It won't be for a liberation movement or a development agenda. If we die, it will be for love, it will be for hope, it will be for reconciliation."

He paused for a moment, not for emphasis, but to really reflect on what he was saying. It went unsaid, but I know his reflection was to think about what Christ would do.

Finally, he nodded and said softly.

"There's no shame in that because it's something worth dying for."

* * *

Dave's philosophy on humanitarian relief would probably fall into the broader category of "white cowboy" as codified by the powers-that-be. In the abstract, I find such models questionable because of the lack of broader coordination and accountability and because of the unequal power dynamics they can perpetuate.

Nonetheless, to me, this honest, humble re-telling of a family's *raison d'être* is at the very core of the Gospel, the "good news" we are meant to share with the world.

And Dave has most certainly shared this good news with others. On this same hillside, I met a cast of local heroes who are laying down their lives for their people each day, willing to sacrifice everything for someone else.

A multi-talented, athletic, extremely humble leader, who can carry half his body weight in a pack for 20-plus miles a day over rough terrain with a beautiful tune and a million-dollar smile on his lips.

A humorous father of four who has somehow simultaneously pastored a vibrant church and led a liberation movement over the past 15 years.

An intellectual from Rangoon who – through careful thought and introspection – decided to exchange his advanced degrees and burgeoning career as a concert pianist for a hard life in the jungle standing with his people.

That names just a few of the courageous souls who are out in that jungle with Dave.

It is beyond doubt that these guys are here for a pressing reason. Though it is hard not to wonder what they might've accomplished were they not needed here, had they been born into a different story.

And thus, I leave this hillside changed – but also confused. *What have I done? What will I do with the gifts, the blessings, the unearned advantages with which I find myself?*

* * *

To be clear, even though I ran around with them in that war zone and tried to lend a hand for some months, I don't know if I can ever aspire to the kind of courage or faith Dave or his fellow rangers embody.

To be clear, I don't think every Christian can or should run around in the jungle like they do. I actually have some major reservations about the trickle-down impacts of this controversial work.

But I count it as one of my life's great, undeserved blessings to have played a tiny, minuscule part in the story being told by these extraordinary lives – and in my first job out of college, no less. Far more than any value I could *add*, I *gained* by virtue of formation within such a community.

What I gained most deeply during those months in the mountains of Northern Myanmar was clarity on *selfish fear* as a key driver of the struggles in my own life and the injustices I see in the world around me.

Courageous men and women like Dave and his rangers also carry fear. But there is a distinction. What sets them apart is that they are not controlled by it.

It was in those mountains with Dave where I first began to distinguish between the innumerable brands of "courage." The ones centered in self-confidence or trust in some physicality, which I had long carried with me, are baseless and as such will eventually crumble.

It was in those mountains with Dave where I first began to realize – if not fully live out the realization – that freedom from fear starts with the little things like refusing to be controlled by a desire for comfort, security, or selfish pleasures. And surely, this is only the beginning.

* * *

In those mountains with Dave, I was – and over a decade later, I remain – at a loss for the steps necessary to build a faith solid enough to rest upon without hesitation. But I do know now that with the years, months, days, or hours I have left on this earth, I hope to discover where such a place of true freedom lies.

A mere glimpse beyond the veil of fear was beginning to revolutionize my life, an uncertain process I hope continues to work its way into my lost and wandering heart as I stumble through this brief existence.

Chapter 30

It's pouring now. Though it has done so a handful of times over the past months, this one is different. You can hear a new voice in the wind, an edge, largely absent from this region for some time. The air holds an increased thickness; the sky an ominous grey which seems determined to stay put. I'm not talking about a chill, or a cold streak, or even a (relatively speaking) cool streak. What I'm referring to – as rainy season makes its abrupt return to this land – is the unmistakable hint of a cycle repeating itself.
My Journal – April 18, 2011

When I arrived, it was rainy season. And now, or if not now, within a few weeks, it will be again. In the interim came a season of cool (again, relatively speaking), and then one of hot, and the cycle continued, entirely unaltered by my presence.

As the rains begin, I run from the house, almost instinctively, to capture a rare opportunity to run in it, to run *with* the rain. I set a new course down unfamiliar streets, exhilarated by the simple pleasure of water, cool natural water, running down my face and body. I am immediately taken with a sublime mix of joy in this moment and excitement for the future. I almost shout out in my exhilaration, but I hold back.

It is in this holding back that I am struck again by the deeper reality of this moment. I am not running *with* the rain after all. I am running in a storm. Yes, water is falling over me. It is affecting my climate, energy, mood, and thoughts. But that car is also in this downpour. And water falls on those buildings just as it does my head. It beads on this dog, just as on my body.

All of a sudden, I am struck again, perhaps for the millionth time this year, with my own finiteness and the gravity of the world around me.

My presence has no aggregate effect on the rain. Sure, I brush it aside from its destiny with earth and sky and earth again. Though, I only delay its course a moment and do so on such a miniscule scale that it is negligible in the long run.

Neither will my presence this year leave a discernible dent in the cycles I came naively to combat. These cycles, these systems of oppression will churn on long after I and the other do-gooders are gone. They have affected me but the impact is not reciprocal.

* * *

I came in naivety. I came to somehow "change the world" in not so many words. And though I certainly did not leave as a jaded, battle-hardened warrior, when I stepped on that plane back to the States, I did so with an incredible sense of awe.

I was struck by the inherent complexity and deep-rooted fear gripping and perpetuating Myanmar's brutal civil war. It sickened me that the people who have the earthly means to make a difference were largely failing to do so – captives of their own Western versions of fear. I left in awe at the gravity of humanity's plight.

These same issues weigh heavy on my heart now. In their light, it is no surprise that I am struck by my own insignificance in what would be a futile attempt to address them. But it is in this recognition of my own insignificance and finiteness that I find encouragement. I know a power greater than these, and I feel certain He empowers His people to do things far beyond their means on behalf of His kingdom.

Fear and callousness and oppression and all the problems of this world weigh heavy on His heart as well. They truly make our Lord sad. Though they distress Him, their complexities, which intimidate us, are inconsequential barriers to the One who made us all.

Yet, if these issues are near to His heart and He has the power to bring about change, why then doesn't He rid us of these ills?

I am coming to believe it is because we were placed here to struggle in this task. He asks us to join Him. He calls us to solidarity – to share in *His* hurt, feel *His* pain, and surrender to *His* passions. And perhaps even more encouraging, He promises a deeper freedom through such surrender.

In my slog through the rain, I was confronted by a new truth. Though my power to influence its course is limited, I am capable of a far greater power. As the rains affect me, I am given emotion, I am given feeling, I am given thought.

If a thought is true, if it is noble, and just, and fair, then perhaps that thought and its resulting action – love – can begin to change the course of this cycle, this oppressive reality of a broken world, this problem too great to tackle on my own.

I left Thailand the next day, fundamentally changed by the rain. Something deep inside me had shaken loose during those months and, perhaps for the first time, I began to glimpse what it might look like to be truly free.

Chapter 31

Love is both something that happens to you and something you decide upon.
Donald Miller, Blue Like Jazz

During my final months in Southeast Asia, an opportunity arose to spend the summer in Northern Pakistan working on a flood relief project. It was a five-month contract which would directly abut the start of my grad program in London, a grand adventure in another distant land. In theory, this sounded amazing.

However, in that moment, my heart longed for a different kind of adventure. Over the course of the journeys and lessons learned overseas, I realized that I'd rather be sharing them.

It wasn't that I was all by myself or lacked friends. But sharing experiences and growth and stupidities and highs and lows with people who likely won't be around next month, next year, or next decade no longer quite satisfied.

Don't get me wrong. Traveling with other folks in those graceful moments where two journeys intersect is a beautiful thing. However, I now sought a journey *with* someone – a journey, together. I longed for someone with whom I could share the road, regardless of which way it turned, regardless of what it did to me.

That someone couldn't be just anyone. It needed to be the right sort of person for whom it would be worth figuring out how to explore this life together, for whom it would be worth slowing down or speeding up or changing course or stopping altogether and turning around. And it had to be someone who felt the same way about me.

Lurking in the back of my mind was the memory of this beautiful and intriguing intern from my time in Colorado who seemed like she might just fit the bill.

Since parting ways at that low-end Mexican restaurant, Rachel and I had kept in touch. It was mostly via email, and for a while it was merely a continuation of our friendship. We continued our lives, dated other people, and occasionally encountered each other via our writing from opposite ends of the world.

Yet as time wore on, I started to wonder whether there might be something more, something worth a diversion back to the US for a few months, just to see.

I asked her to Skype, told her how I felt, and invited her on a date upon my return. Hesitantly, she accepted; just one date and we'd see where it went from there.

For me, this was all the encouragement I needed. I didn't know what the summer would hold, but running around the Karakoram of Northern Pakistan could come later if things didn't work out. So, back to Colorado I went.

I arrived a few days before her birthday, and she was gracious enough to allow me to spend the day with her.

While I was away, we had a running joke that she was going to show up and visit me on one of my adventures. So, with our date, we "re-visited" some of my highlights from the preceding year.

"Myanmar" was an intense morning hike outside Colorado Springs since most of my time in-country was spent in the mountains. I didn't ask her to carry a 45lb pack. I did, however, bring along breakfast which I laid out by a stream near the crux of the hike for us to enjoy after the workout.

"Thailand" was a Thai restaurant where I'd befriended the owner with my limited knowledge of her language and home country. Earlier in the week, I'd convinced Mae to let me use her kitchen to make Rachel *panang* curry and *som tom* for lunch.

There were a few other stops in there, but I kindly spared her my "Malaysia" experience of failing at public transportation. We would save that one for our sixth anniversary, "romantically" running down an inter-city bus hand-in-hand in the fading light outside Medellin, Colombia. But I'm getting ahead of myself.

Our first date was quickly followed by a second. We watched the Beatles inspired musical, *Across the Universe*. Despite mixed reviews in the box office, I recall the movie as uniquely inspired and beautiful. This may or may not have had something to do with the person sitting next to me.

The most memorable scene in the movie for me, the moment which still flashes back to mind when I recall it today, was James Sturgess' soaring, soothing, soulful rendition of the title song.

* * *

Living, breathing, feeling fully in the present moment is exceedingly difficult for me. But with this plot line, this singer, these words, and this woman by my side, there was, in this moment, nothing else.

* * *

As the film drew to its epic close with all the main characters crooning from an East Side rooftop, I somehow knew there would be a third date and a fourth and maybe, hopefully, a great many more.

Love itself was not yet fully formed, but the intellectual recognition and physical attraction began to merge our paths that evening as we sat on the very edge of a clearing and prepared to take our first steps together.

The summer with Rachel was a beautiful blur, a time in the warm Colorado sun which changed and redirected my life in ways I would never have expected and now can't imagine living without.

There was still that small matter of grad school in the fall.

Yet five months later, as plane wheels lifted me off US soil once again, I left my heart behind.

I was on my own path no longer.

Chapter 32

Nothing is certain in London but expense.
William Shenstone, 1743

My grad school packing list included a backpack full of clothes, a backpack full of camping gear, and a backpack full of books.

A more practical choice might have been a single suitcase and a carry-on backpack of books. Yet, the moment you trade your pack for a suitcase, you are no longer an authentic traveler... or some similar logic.

For me, in this very moment in my life, practical was synonymous with sell-out. I felt I'd found my identity as a "backpacker with purpose" or some other narcissistic, millennial identifier.

It's 5:45am when I collect this ensemble from Heathrow at the end of my red-eye, drag it half-way to the Underground and summarily quit.

It was another 400 yards to the Underground entrance. Then, I needed to figure out the "Tube" and take the District Line 45 minutes to Sloan Square. Finally, I'd have to walk close to a mile to my lodging for the night.

Or... I could shlep my bags 50 yards to the right and hop in a taxi. It was a 9-mile ride. In Thailand, the only place I'd ever taken a taxi, that equaled, what, $3 max? New identity be damned. This was no decision at all.

Hopping out at the door, I was in for my first London surprise. £60 GBP or about $100 USD.

That was $100 USD plus exchange fees, compounded at 5.8% interest annually no less. I was certifiably broke, and it was student loan money from here on out.

London lands its first punch.

* * *

I hit back hard in my fight against the pound sterling – at the very hazy line I was straddling between impetuous vagrant and adventurous intellectual – when I landed my first flat.

My arbitrary student budget allowed a combined £400 per month for British pubs and shoestring travel beyond British borders but a paltry £300 for rent. If you've ever been to London, you'll appreciate the utter laugh-ability of such a "plan."

Truly, it should have been impossible. Yet in Jonathan, I stumbled upon a roommate as determinedly cheap as myself and in Ben, a host willing to put up with two stupid, miserly Americans in his lovely little Fulham flat.

Jonathan and I shared the 8x8 foot second bedroom in Ben's place that year. It was just big enough for one twin mattress and one camping pad. So, we split the academic year. Fall semester. Jonathan got the mattress and I slept on the pad on the ground. Spring semester, we switched.

I'd strike again in my quixotic battle against London's exorbitance in my mode of transport. At 75mpg, my aging, £300 Honda CB500 motorcycle shaved my daily commute costs from £7.50 on the tube to £0.30 in gas. That incredible ratio of fun per pound-sterling also transformed my ability to explore Europe and the UK on a paltry budget. I sold the bike at the end of the year – after 7,000 additional miles and one oil change worth of maintenance – for £500, making it one of the great investments in automotive history.

In the end, London would win this battle, with me $50,000 devalued US dollars in the hole. But no one could say I didn't put up a good fight.

* * *

I was saving every penny for a reason. I aimed to get out of

London at least twice a month, and England at least once.

Some weekends, I'd take the bike into the lush, rolling, British countryside or out to the wild Welsh coast. Once I even took it across the channel to France.

Some weekends, I'd book Ryanair's cheapest flights, picking a destination matching my budget. Using this approach, I spent long weekends in Porto, Portugal; Valencia, Spain; and Turin, Italy; amongst others averaging $50 roundtrips each.

Other weekends, I'd make plans to meet friends in far flung reaches of the continent – in Hungary and East Germany and, yes, glorious Latvia.

Monthly at least, I'd ride through the wind and rain to Oxford for research with a professor there, to study in the Bodleian Library, to immerse in the palpably rich intellectual history amidst those dreaming spires.

* * *

With all that movement, I was still in London every Tuesday through Thursday for classes. Such a routine was only possible within a UK system of education which holds markedly different values from ours stateside.

I bucked and butted heads with the US pedagogical machine from the age of five until I graduated from college at 22. My restless spirit, hyperactive body, and unruly mind rejected the daily six-hour imprisonment. I learned begrudgingly, force-fed whatever was put on my plate. I didn't feel I needed to complete assignment after mindless assignment to learn, and I didn't respond well to the stifling nature of constant assessment.

I learn best – as many do – via immersion in material, finding tangible ways to experience and bring to life challenging concepts and when offered space to discuss and debate and dialogue with classmates, professors, and sojourners alike.

For my time in and around London, the UK system offered

me this educational experience. It also surrounded me with peers and professors who challenged me and helped open doors to continue exploring the areas which most piqued my growing intellectual curiosity.

Each weekend on the road, I was no longer just exploring and traveling. I was reading and writing voraciously. I was seeing the lessons from my – often soggy and windblown – books play out in the real world. I was testing my theories and ideas about that real world in the libraries, pubs, hostels, and trails of the great European melting pot.

In a word – for the first time in my life, as I bucked and writhed against the inevitability of London's expense – I was learning.

* * *

As I learned, however, I continued to seek something I would never find over books and beers in a London pub or on the back of a motorcycle with the wind racing through my unkempt hair.

I was still missing out on the present, on the good life which can flow from immersion in one's physical and relational place. Instead, I fled the city and fought daily over each miserable tuppence.

I was still striving to approximate my identity through a now familiar set of lost and wandering means. I was the rent-seeking shoestring backpacker-cum-humanitarian, the self-minted rogue intellectual chasing "freedom" – the full weight and glory of the "pinnacle" pressing me ever onward in pursuit of God knows what.

Chapter 33

Believing you're a good person and actually being one are two completely different things.
Anonymous

It's 3:00am. I wake from a deep sleep as the cabin lights come on in the business class section of the 747 and the captain announces we are beginning our initial descent into Jomo Kenyatta International.

No, this is not a fantasy flash-forward to 2050. I'm not the fat, rich businessman or pretentious World Bank staffer I never dreamt of becoming. Still a poor, skinny grad-student, now en route to Nairobi for dissertation research.

So why am I lounging in business class? Good question.

From 2010–2014, I took over 50 international flights. On exactly 11 of these flights, I boarded in a certain, special mood. The technical term, I believe, is "cocky."

I'd decide that for whatever reason, I thought I could be confident and charming enough to get something I wanted.

What I wanted was a good night's sleep.

I'd watch the flight attendants and try to identify the very nicest, most accommodating looking one. Then, I'd walk up, introduce myself, apologize "for the inconvenience" and then boldly proclaim that I was a famous singer or actor who had been incorrectly booked in coach "by my agent."

"I normally wouldn't care, but these folks (points vaguely), are bothering me for my autograph and I really need to get some sleep. We have a big (show/scene/etc.) starting right when we land."

At some point along the way, I had heard that once the doors were closed, there was no mechanism to officially upgrade people (and thus charge them). So, I'd generally wait until right

157

when the doors were closing to make my ask.

On 9 of the 11 times I pulled this little stunt, I was immediately ushered into business class with no questions asked. This – my first flight to the African continent, to study and learn about the great inequities of privilege which separate lives like mine from a more common experience – was one of those times.

* * *

The next leg of my journey was decidedly not business class.

The bus departing Nairobi for the Ugandan border wasn't so much a bus as it was a 12-passenger van which, on this particular voyage, would ultimately accommodate 21 adult passengers, 3 babies, and a chicken or two.

I was the first passenger to board at around 6:30am. I asked the driver when we'd depart. He flatly responded, "when full."

There was no departure time, no schedule. When the bus finally filled up at 7:15am, I figured that was it: onward to Busia.

Instead, the bus would stop every 10–15 minutes, let folks out, and then wait until it filled back up.

The 300-mile trip took nearly 10.5 hours. It was absolute misery. It also remains ingrained as one of my favorite travel memories.

It wasn't an open-bed truck, but I had the window seat in the very back, and when the dust wasn't so bad, I'd stick my head out into the wind in pure bliss.

* * *

The plan was to meet Willy, a Ugandan friend from Compassion, at the border, but my phone had no service. I called him using a borrowed cell back in Nairobi and gave him an approximate arrival time. We were 4 hours past that now, and I held no hope he would be there. I had literally no idea what I would do, and it was getting dark.

As we pulled up to the border, I hopped off the bus and paid my fare, $1.50. I looked around for a few seconds and then saw Willy running up to me.

For the previous three hours, he'd been asking people crossing the border if they'd passed a white guy in any of the chicken buses coming from Nairobi. One lady in an SUV said she had, so he perched by the side of the road and waited for me.

We crossed the chaotic-looking overland border into Uganda with no issue whatsoever. Willy seemed to know everyone.

The next day, Willy drove me to an open lot near his home in Busia. We got out of his truck, and he handed me a shovel. He asked me to dig into the ground while he took my picture.

He then explained that this was the site of the new social enterprise he was starting and that he'd been waiting to have the construction crew commence work until I came to break the ground.

I was overwhelmed and humbled. In the months leading up to the trip, I had helped Willy with a few projects as he got his new organization off the ground. But I had viewed these as favors to an old friend, not the beginning of a business partnership.

Willy had different ideas and, in his own subtle, loving, persuasive way, won me over. Thus would my second job begin.

In the near term, my brief time with Willy in Busia helped ground a once wandering, highly abstract dissertation into a focused baseline assessment studying the curricular and programmatic needs a project (perhaps one like Willy's) might require in order to be successful and impactful, given the situation in the area.

Over the next four years, I would serve as the project's first Director of Operations, helping to manage the finances, donor relations, and programming while working with Willy to build a team who could take the organization to the next level.

Today, Willy's "Give Hope" campuses offer a quality education to hundreds of students while sustainably subsidizing on-site housing and tuition for vulnerable children through various livelihood projects. It has been one of the greatest privileges of my life to stumble into involvement with this work and to labor alongside Willy in the beautiful story of this organization.

It is crazy to me that Willy wanted my help or that what I brought to the table – my confused, impure motives and almost non-existent knowledge of school operations or local context – was able to contribute to a positive impact on these kids' lives.

* * *

In this way, I can look back on my self-reflective, even overtly self-serving time in grad school – the pubs and travels and libraries and arrogant business class upgrades – and see some whispers of meaning infused at a level far beyond my ability to orchestrate.

Chapter 34

Cyclists see considerably more of this beautiful world than any other class of citizens. A good bicycle, well applied, will cure most ills this flesh is heir to.

Dr K.K. Doty, Nineteenth-Century New Yorker and cycling evangelist

With the primary data needed for my dissertation in-hand, I returned to London for a brief visit with my aunt, uncle and cousin Chris. When his mom and dad left town, Chris and I hopped on a plane to Shannon Airport in Western Ireland.

Our plan was simple: meet Padraic at the airport and go from there.

Padraic came to the terminal with two touring bicycles, pannier bags and a map. For $400 each, the steeds were ours for a month.

It was raining when we started, but the bags were waterproof and the air was warm, so we started riding.

Perhaps it was my Irish family heritage, perhaps it was the promise of plentiful Guinness down the road, or perhaps it was the magical, misty green all around me, but I fell in love with the place the moment my feet hit the peddles.

We rode to the coast and turned north that day. As the light grew dim, we rolled into the village of Labasheeda, County Clare. Labasheeda boasted but a single pub, which we quickly located.

Within a few minutes a big man named Quinn had welcomed us, told us about his cousins in Boston, bought us each a pint, and offered us a field to pitch our tent for the night.

This, more or less, was the story of our time in Ireland. It is also the story of my dissertation, the vast majority of which was drafted as Chris read or slept in that tent in various national parks and farmers' fields as well as in lively pubs across West Ireland's charming, idyllic villages.

For the next few weeks, we biked up and down the West Coast – to the cliffs of Moher and the little village of Doolin, to the great seaside mountain range of Connemara, to Galway for a music festival, to the Aran Islands, to Cork and Killarney and Dingle Peninsula, and, of course, up the castle to kiss the Blarney Stone.

Chris eventually returned via Shannon Airport, and I decided to bike across the interior to Dublin where my own journey would end. That glorious month, I logged just shy of 1,000 miles and 10,000 rather uninspired written words.

I wonder if it was the nature of bike travel that made it so visceral, so perfect, so healing and almost meaningful. Or perhaps it was the people, so welcoming, warm, and immediately familiar. Regardless the reason, in all my travels, I've never felt so at peace, so at ease, so present, so delighted with every moment, with every up and down, with every cool, rainy night and warm, cozy pub as on that trip – though the next week came close.

* * *

After bidding farewell to Ireland, I returned the bike and flew from Dublin to London. By now I knew the Underground well. No exorbitant taxis on this trip.

I took the District Line straight to Westminster where I met my old college buddy Klossy, and a good friend from grad school Ginger Matt.

I'd lured these two great guys into doing a special hike with me. We took a train up to Carlisle near the Scottish border and then a taxi over to tiny Bowness-on-Solway where England and Scotland converge on the rugged edge of the Irish Sea.

It was my last week in the UK. As something of a dramatic

conclusion, I wanted to "walk across the country." Conveniently, England is made for just such adventures and there happens to be a trail running the gorgeous border of England and Scotland called Hadrian's Wall.

The 2,000-year-old wall defines the northernmost boundary of the Holy Roman Empire, named after the emperor who oversaw the ancient imperial powerhouse at its most expansive.

For us, the "wall" brought with it more than its fair share of memories and silly conquests. For four days and nearly 100 miles, we goaded and peer pressured each other on our journey over the bucolic terrain – playing "tag" with sheep, running in full-pack terror from gangs of angry cows, and regaling locals in every pub along the way with the tales of our exploits.

As the sun set on our final day, we limped down the hill into Newcastle-Upon-Tyne and stumbled into a warm, welcoming pub. We grabbed dinner, and I downed my first ever Newcastle beer. If you haven't tried one, I'll tell you they are as terrible at the source as anywhere else in the world. Just awful stuff.

We trained back to London the next day and rode laps on the Underground until it shut down – playing guitar, making up silly songs about each other, and re-living the glory of the hike in typically obnoxious fashion.

I flew back to the States the next morning, still smiling from the fun, but mostly ready to submit my dissertation and begin the next chapter of life.

* * *

I'd spent the last four years on just such adventures, traveling extensively, formally and informally learning about myself and about life beyond the wealthy western world. I was gaining nuanced, experience-informed opinions (if nothing more) about why poor countries and poor people are poor, what can and should be done to attempt to re-balance the inequities, and what works and what really, truly doesn't.

Wrestling with these and other critical yet unanswerable questions had become a central part of my identity. As much as I knew these questions were important and timely and interesting, I was also drawn further in my interest because of what their pursuit said about me.

I'd gotten into an elite grad school and excelled beyond expectation in my courses. *This had to say something, mean something about me, right?*

Equally important as the fact that I was excelling, was *what* I was excelling at, along with *how* and *where* I was living my life. After all these years and experiences, the question of *who* I was really becoming still escaped me.

What (I was doing/thinking/etc.), *how* (crazy the story) and *where* (I was going) were the metrics by which I measured my value and approximated my identity.

I took pride in the fact that I had bucked the system and given up a somewhat lucrative career in accounting to chart my own destiny.

I was relieved that I could excuse, even elevate, my lack of a formal, linear resume because of the gravity of the line of work with which I was flirting.

I enjoyed that *almost* everyone in my life found what I was doing interesting even though I suspected most wouldn't really enjoy this life in practice.

I loved that I was charting my own path, that I was doing something I found important, that I was in small ways succeeding, and that, with an ever-mounting body of proof, others recognized and validated the identity I was building for myself.

It wasn't that I didn't actually care about what I was doing.

I did and do care deeply about the plight of the world's most vulnerable.

I did and do believe more people should care and that a shift in thinking and action is necessary if our Church hopes to be a voice for the voiceless.

I did and do feel authentically liberated and free and at home and at peace on the road with no plan and little control over what happens next.

But I also cared (and care) deeply about being (and being viewed as) competent in the pursuit of whatever crazy identity I was and am constructing for my life.

When such is your focus, it is all too easy to lose track of what is truly important.

Sometimes, that is. Other times, a vision for what *should be, must be*, is just too clear to miss, even for a stumbling fool like me.

Chapter 35

Give every day the chance to become the most beautiful of your life.
Mark Twain

It is difficult to explain those beautiful dreams upon waking. One cannot adequately grasp the colors, the feelings, the perfection – unless experienced. But I shall take a chance with mine; in the hope that you might catch a glimpse of the beauty, love, and inspiration whispered over us on that day in April.

I had her thoroughly convinced that a commitment of such magnitude was still a long way off, and, therefore, would surely NOT occur during her trip to visit me in England that spring.

We hadn't seen each other in months. I brought flowers to the airport, and as she took them, it took me a few extra seconds to reconcile the fact that we were no longer staring at images on a screen, but into each other's eyes.

* * *

It was a Sunday, the first of April, and without question the most perfect, happiest day of my life. The air was crisp, the sky cerulean. We picked up some sandwiches and wound up at a dock. Not just any dock, but *the* dock leading to Magdalen College's back gardens.

Magdalen was the College at Oxford where C.S. Lewis taught, meaningful for our mutual love of his work. I rented a punt boat and propelled us through the peaceful, almost mystical gardens.

We floated past banks of wildflowers, under ancient bridges, finding ourselves at the tri-county line between Narnia, the Shire, and Never Never Land. I munched on an apple and stated that this was my most favorite day of the trip. She said the same.

After a little while, we tied our boat to a sapling and crawled up the bank to a little meadow. We talked amidst the dew-covered flowers and dreamed of a life of such joys as each other's company from here on out.

Later, as we walked barefoot through the gardens, she bent down to pick a flower. When she looked back up, I was on my knee.

* * *

To say that day, that moment, changed my life is an understatement and an overstatement at the same time. A day like that, a day of such perfection, does not come about without many other, harder days. It is followed by and even promises harder days as well.

Days like this are built from the mysterious dance of lives moving in unison toward each other, toward growing commitment and relationship and love. In such a light, it is no surprise that I count this day as the happiest of my life.

Amidst years of struggling and striving and stumbling in pursuit of my own purposes, this day for me and for her was a representation of an authentic pursuit of something greater, something higher.

I was only at the beginning of an awareness of this higher meaning that day. In many ways I still am.

Just a week later, I was on that plane pretending to be a rockstar to get a business class upgrade on my first flight to Africa, proving as always that one step forward in my moral journey is almost always followed by at least a few hops back.

Nonetheless, in those gardens I began to realize – if only imperfectly – that, in the end, the freedom I seek is not a loosening of bonds, nor is it further individuation or a life of ultimate choice and liberty on the road riding free with my hair blowing in the wind.

True freedom is not about getting to choose, but learning how to choose well.

Four and a half months later, after the chicken bus, and the ground-breaking in Uganda, and the dissertation, and the bike across Ireland, and the walk across Scotland, I chose again. We made our vows and forever bound ourselves to each other, no longer free to be merely individuals.

Years after, I look back – past all the stumbling failures and unforeseen hardships and tiny victories, and hard won, easily lost moral steps forward – to that moment.

Without doubt, I hold that day in Magdalen when I chose relationship with another as my most important decision, my highest priority, and my longest commitment, as my life's defining joy and greatest freedom.

Section 5

On being together

Chapter 36

The only way to thrive in marriage is to become a better person –
more patient, wise, compassionate, persevering, communicative,
and humble.
David Brooks, The Second Mountain

We're flying up the left coast now. Hours ago, we left San
Francisco behind, and it's all winding curves and dramatic
vistas from here to Portland. We stay at an inn overlooking the
Sonoma coast one night and a historic riverfront hotel the next.
We go for runs amidst the mighty redwoods and discover tiny
coves and inlets.

We drive up the famed Highway 101: Cabos San Lucas to
Portland. Well, we skip a few of the middle miles in-flight, but
who's counting. We're together.

A spontaneous life on the road takes on new meaning as
it offers up opportunity to deepen relationship with another
– another so kind and loving and beautiful that I find myself
reflecting upon my good fortune more often than normal this
trip.

* * *

A month after returning from our honeymoon, we head back
to the UK for a contract job I'll work while continuing to help
Willy with his project.

In the first real act of self-sacrificial love of our marriage,
Rachel left her life in Colorado to be with me.

She is contemplating a career shift and grad school, but still.
In that moment of her leaving, of giving up the life she'd made
there these last three years, I am sad. Something just doesn't
feel right, seeing her uproot herself like that for no better reason

than our (mostly my) desire for a life abroad.

I remember hoping and praying I might one day be able to do the same for her. In that hoping and praying I began to wrestle – for the first time – with the moral clarity of the life I'd been leading.

Up to this point, I'd always seen it as pretty black and white.

On one hand, you have people who are clinging to security, safety, the easy way out; they "settle," pick a city, buy a home, pursue a "normal" career, cave to hollow materialism, and shift their lives under the weight of those great American idols.

Then, on the other hand, you have people who buck the system, who resist the fear of instability and an uncertain future; who give up control over outcomes; who trust in what they believe to be God or the universe or the holy power of the open road and surrender to life "the way we were meant to live." People like me, of course.

But now I begin to question, begin to wonder. There must be more.

Perhaps, there is something to this idea of place, this concept of community, this surrender to a life which trades some of that ultimate freedom for deeper, tighter bonds.

But I know better. I've seen how "community" and "place" and "home" are words weak people use to justify a weak life, an easy way.

Still, something doesn't feel quite right this time about me being the force which rips Rachel's developing roots away from this soil. Perhaps, I tell myself, that's just because I love her and I know she's sad in a way, though she barely shows it.

* * *

In any case, we go. We load all our stuff into a 5x10 storage unit and head to England.

After all my years on the road, I finally have a paying job in another country. I feel somehow validated by this fact; surely this means I (and we) should be here.

Living in England this second time – with the love of my life – is, frankly, difficult. We're in a small village on the outskirts of London and everything is so expensive that we have to rent the upstairs of someone's house. It is not ideal.

But we are together. For now, that is enough.

And we still have the joy of travel, together. That fall, we visit Oxford and Cambridge and lovely Bath. We see plays in London and explore the city. We travel to lush, rolling western Ireland and the mazed city of Istanbul.

Things are going well at my new job and for a moment it looks like we might find roots across the pond. We finally find a nice flat in West London and scrape together money for a deposit.

At that very moment a wrench is thrown. My contract is unexpectedly not renewed.

But why should I worry? I miraculously have a job offer that would base us in Southeast Asia after a year at "HQ." Never mind that "HQ" is in Colorado... where we just left.

I scarcely think about the fact that Rachel would be giving up grad school in London, uprooting again for nothing but my own wandering path. But she is up for it. What I fail to see in her openness is a deep driving desire for what is best for me above and beyond her own preferences.

As I pen these words, my heart breaks again under the weight of my own selfishness.

In the moment, it was no decision. A chance to move *again*. A chance to spend time in Colorado and then live *with* Rachel in Southeast Asia working in *my* field, aligned with *my* identity.

Surely, this was *my* destiny, or so *I* imagined.

* * *

So confident was I in this vision for our future that I suggested we – now jobless and well into six figures of student loan debt – maximize our remaining weeks in Europe.

We use that deposit money for a last-second jaunt to the gorgeous northern Italian coastal villages of Cinque Terre. We stay in a 400-year-old apartment overlooking the sea on this brand-new site called Airbnb. We pass a somehow carefree week from this venue – trekking between the towns and vineyards and eating the best pizza of our lives amidst one of the world's most intoxicating blends of natural and human-created beauty.

Then, suddenly, our break with reality is over and we are on a flight back to the US. A badly needed adjustment in my life outlook is just around the corner. I am not prepared for what is coming.

Chapter 37

The hardest thing to learn in life is which bridge to cross and which to burn.
Bertrand Russell

We arrived back in Colorado jobless, homeless, buried in over $100,000 of student debt – but we were full of hope. Rachel had plenty of connections in town and I was heading for a dream job.

Our third day back, all that hope fell apart. I learned that funding for the job had been pulled last minute and that my offer was contingent on that funding. No job.

Up to this moment, I'd always held employment pretty loosely. I was charting my own path after all, punching my own ticket. And honestly, that's a relatively easy thing to do under certain circumstances.

At the "pinnacle," with no debt, no responsibilities, no ties, you have the flexibility, the leverage even, to pick and choose what you want to do and let the rest roll off your back.

Such an approach is liberating and empowering in many ways. It is also a little bit like continuing to be a child. The only way you can ever hope to maintain such a life is to vehemently reject any force which might bind you, "tie you down" or, in other words, heap responsibilities and force maturity into your selfish, privileged life. The longer you resist, the harder it hits when reality finally drops.

In that moment, reality hit me like an anvil from the stratosphere.

In an instant, for the first time in my life, employment shifted from just something everyone did, something I did somewhat begrudgingly, with a chip on my shoulder – and on which I placed only moderate value – to something I absolutely needed, something *we* needed.

Work became a requisite condition for survival. In that shift, I grazed the rough outer rim of the privileged bubble in which I'd lived for so long.

But as much as this moment was a depressing reckoning with my own mortality and the finite limits of my ability, it was also the beginning of becoming the man I was meant to be.

In that moment when I realized I needed a job (any job) to get by, I found something of a calling as a co-provider for a family. I assumed responsibility for the debt I'd accumulated in grad school. I accepted for the first time a shared burden with Rachel for the debt she had also accrued in college.

It was a tough stretch. I applied to literally every job opening I could find. After two months, all I'd landed were offers to work as a bank teller and a server at a local brewery. Nothing against such career tracks, but neither job represented a sustainable situation for people under as much debt-by-degree as we.

Nonetheless, I had to accept them both. We'd been living off credit cards and needed employment. Rachel picked up freelance work and together, we were able to stay afloat... but we were treading water.

Then after another painful two months, I found a more permanent solution.

I *happened* to have a friend working for a small tech company in DC. This company was working in the wedding and events space; it wasn't exactly my MO, but she was able to get me an interview. When I flew out, I *happened* to meet the COO who *happened* to think highly of my grad school and we *happened* to really hit it off. We met up for beers that evening and he *happened* to have another, better role in mind for someone like me.

At the end of this long string of good fortune, he offered me a job leading their Strategic Partnerships and International Expansion Division – a soon to be Division of 1.

I can't say I was thrilled about moving from International

Development to an events industry tech start-up. However, starting pay was decent with significant upside potential, and I had literally no other options. Also, I could keep working a few evenings a week at that brewery.

* * *

Over the next few years, as we buckled down to rid ourselves of the nasty burden of debt, something pretty crazy happened in those two companies.

The brewery grew from a home brewer and a few servers working out of a strip mall store to one of the highest grossing breweries in the state of Colorado – itself one of the true emerging meccas of the craft beer craze.

That little tech company grew even more. I joined a team of around 80 which was operating in one country with annual revenue around $6 million. When I left several years later, it was the undisputed industry leader – employing over 1,000 staff in 26 countries with operating revenue in the hundreds of millions.

I could look back on that explosive growth which defined those years for us and elevated us out of debt as a testament to my work ethic, my business acumen, or to some cult-like belief in the "power of positive thinking." I could see my role in that epic corporate rise as a validation of those subtle myths we all want desperately to believe about ourselves; that we are special and uniquely gifted and harder working and thus, somehow, predestined for our place at the "pinnacle."

And certainly, I did play a part in the success of those organizations. I'm not blind to that reality either.

But those companies were ascendent, and I simply had the opportunity to be along for the ride because I came with the right type of pedigree and mentality and was in the right place at the right time.

And to what do I attribute this grand coincidence? God's providence?

Yes, but that is – at best – an oversimplification and – at worst – the beginning of a grossly misleading tale, the conclusion of which only deepens confusion and self-deception.

The facts are: I was in that place at that time with those skills and credentials because I was given, from birth, more than most and more than I deserve and probably more than is spiritually healthy in terms of material advantages.

In many senses, I was born – as a white, precocious male, from a stable, loving American family – with just about everything I needed to capitalize on these opportunities when they inevitably came knocking.

With those advantages, the material world was always mine to lose. That doesn't mean I was guaranteed victory. But assuredly, any victory I did win would, in some way or another, be won with a significant head start on the vast majority of global, historical humanity. Moreover, because of that privileged position, any failure would leave no one to blame but myself.

Ultimately, I found the whole endeavor entirely unsatisfying.

Perhaps, it was because of the high-risk, low-reward narrative lens with which I viewed the corporate ladder.

Perhaps, it was because *that job* was so far away from what I thought I wanted to be doing or how I wanted to be viewed that it felt embarrassing.

Perhaps, it was because I was still so desperately fixated on customizing, maximizing my identity based on my own idea of what my life should be about.

Regardless the reason, given my privileged upbringing and the myriad options afforded me, the traditional markers of success which kept piling up – title increases and bonus checks and expanding empire and luxurious work events and first class travel never held much sway.

Four years and four months after entering this world, I

Chapter 37

would leave it again. I was grateful for the financial freedom those years provided but happy, okay, almost desperate to get off this path.

This decision wasn't primarily a moral one. I was and am under no delusions that walking away from money inherently made me better or more intelligent or more ethical than those who make the opposite choice. Were it a simple matter of right vs. wrong, I likely would've chosen the latter.

For me though, internally, I always hoped it was only a matter of time before I'd turn my back on the corporate world for good. I kept my eyes open, and when the right opportunity opened up, I knew it would never be a choice at all.

* * *

It was a few years later when that opportunity arose. I was in Mexico City helping orchestrate a strategic commercial shift into the booming Latin American market.

Or, presumably, that's what I was doing.

I'd had my meetings and done my work, but my heart was elsewhere.

On Friday afternoon, I ditched my sport coat and khakis and suitcase full of corporate nonsense at the concierge of my five-star hotel and threw a grungy change of clothes into an aging, well-worn backpack.

I hopped in a bus and headed out of town, chatting away excitedly in broken Spanish with my fellow riders. When this bus reached Xonacatlán, I hopped on a smaller bus which wound deep into the mountains.

My vague plan was to climb the mighty Nevado de Toluca, one of the 20 tallest mountains in North America. In reality, that's where my plans started and ended.

I needed this burst of spontaneity and adventure just to see me through what I increasingly viewed as the planned

179

monotony and meaningless existence of profit-driven office life.

That afternoon, I hiked 10 miles up to a cabaña near the summit and pondered what might lie ahead.

Rachel was applying to grad school and I was eager to support her in this venture as she had once supported me a few years prior.

Somewhat more selfishly, I was more than ready to flee the life I was currently living in my corporate job.

I reached the cabaña at last light and paid my $5 for a twin cot.

I slept like a baby and woke to a clear morning on the edge of a crater, looking down into a crystal blue mountain lake and up to crags soaring nearly 16,000 feet above sea level.

After a quick breakfast, I started to pick my way up the spires. Slowly, carefully, patiently, always up. As the rhythm of the climb developed, I slipped back into thoughts of what might be.

We'd visited a prestigious university in a college town that autumn and fallen in love with its campus and the slower pace of life outside the city. Rachel had applied, and we'd begun to dream about how we might transition to such a life.

Aimlessly searching the job boards, I found out that this little college just *happened* to host a USAID Global Development Lab – a humanitarian consultancy of sorts. They conducted policy research and served as advisors to USAID, the UN, the World Bank – trying to help the big guys send their money to the right places to help the poorest people.

This sounded like a research agenda right up my alley but the question remained. Why would they want to work with someone who had been out of the field for nearly four years and had gained little practical expertise to speak of in the years prior?

I applied nonetheless and had actually interviewed the week prior. What if?

Even still, it was impossible. I knew the types of candidates they were seeking, and I just didn't fit. I was fairly sure I could do the job, but I had little confidence I would get the offer.

* * *

I'd made it to the top. Looking out over the crater and the valley below was inspiring. But, as usual on such peaks, the inspiration I felt was not actually one of self-satisfied conquest.

Deeper, more authentically, I was inspired by an urge: the urge to climb another mountain. It was not purely a "grass is greener" sort of urge – though that was undeniably a key part. It was also a shift, a redefinition of purpose, and a honing of focus on the next challenge, hopefully one at least slightly more oriented toward others' good than my own.

I was ready for my next mountain.

* * *

On my way down, I befriended some college kids out for the weekend from Mexico City. They offered me a ride back to town and took me to an amazing spot for lunch overlooking the city.

By the time I got back to the hotel – joyfully full of maiz, mole, and mezcal – I'd all but forgotten about the job. Time to focus up for another week of suits and meetings and negotiations and money. I'd dream of the future another day.

But then, waiting in my inbox, I found an offer letter.

Three weeks later, we were moving south to start the next chapter of our journey, our next mountain together.

Chapter 38

*It is a chaotic mixture of tribes large and small. Artificial man-
made borders cannot contain historic conflicts and rivalries. Inter-
marriage is rare, incest within the group common, as are predatory
raids. It is a cash culture, but also one of barter. A variety of
dialects – too many to count – are spoken. I'm describing, of course,
the international aid community, and especially the development
professionals who work in Africa.*

Alexander Wooley, disgruntled aid worker, journalist, friend

Exactly one year after that Mexican mountain top, I found
myself on another mountain of sorts. The view was a bit less
pristine, but equally as breathtaking.

This mountain was actually a hillside overlooking Monrovia,
Liberia.

On top of this hillside I stood, perched on the roof of one of
Africa's most luxurious hotels, or what remains of it at least. In
1990, Charles Taylor and his rebels – the most famous in a long
string of post-colonial demons which have haunted this country
since its birth – ransacked the place.

My "tour" of the once grand Ducor Hotel was $2 cash
payable to the security guard who makes $5 per day from the
government to keep people out.

Today, the venue sits looted, gutted, and abandoned. Every
item of even marginal value – elevators, handrails, furniture,
carpets, fixtures, lights, wallpaper, drywall, even most of the
nails and screws – is long since scavenged. Former opulence is
replaced with graffiti and the putrid evidence of now-evicted
squatters. The walk up the 20 flights of stairs to this rooftop is
downright eerie.

Ducor Hotel stands as a reminder of Liberia's brutal past and
its bleak future. Gazing out over the Atlantic, you – all too easily

– look directly over a small strip of land, filled with jumbled, crooked buildings and unpaved roads, hundreds of feet below.

Small, lowly West Point is one of the poorest neighborhoods in the poorest country in the world. It was ground zero for the Ebola crisis which crippled Liberia a few years prior and is an unmitigated humanitarian crisis on a good day.

Looking across the street in the other direction, you peer right into the sprawling, highly secure cement compound of the US Embassy. By some estimates, 95% of Liberia's GDP comes from foreign aid, the largest portion of which originates on US soil. This is a sad state of affairs, but it is the world in which we live. A withdrawal or even a sizable reduction of this assistance in its various forms would undoubtedly plunge the country into anarchy, epidemic, and brutal violence within months.

I am here as a small part of this messy, poorly administered, highly politicized, inefficient, totally necessary industry. My team's role this week is to lead a series of trainings for a UN-funded inter-agency taskforce on how to improve transparency and accountability in the country's notoriously corrupt natural resources sector.

That morning was an odd and not so odd one for me. I gave a morning interview for UNMIL Radio discussing what the evidence suggests corporations profiting off Liberia's vast natural resources are doing to help the impoverished nation.

Slightly worse than nothing is the simple answer, though few things are simple here.

Twenty minutes later, I was arrested for "taking the wrong kind of taxi" to a training event across town. I couldn't quite stomach paying the bribe this time, so I got hauled off to the local jail for a morning of harmless intimidation.

Once booked, I asked to call the US consulate. The officers let me out of the cell to make the call. Oddly, they left me unattended in the lobby. The call didn't go through. After sitting there for 10 minutes, I walked outside.

No cops anywhere. It was lunch hour.

Somewhat relieved and a bit annoyed, I flagged down another taxi and arrived at the training about an hour late.

Later that afternoon, after leaving Ducor Hotel's rooftop, I met two of my colleagues and a local friend for dinner at a pizza place. To our right sat none other than Yormie Johnson surrounded by three bodyguards.

Yormie is better known as "Prince" Johnson. As Charles Taylor's former right-hand man, Prince J is best known for the brutal, graphic video taken of him cutting off the ear of former Liberian President Samuel Doe and then shooting him to death while laughing and sipping a Bud Light. Today, he is a Liberian Senator and frequents this pizza place, apparently.

I arrive back at my hotel disturbed and a bit mystified at how I've found myself on this new mountain of sorts. As I nod off, I try to shake off the weight of these questions for a moment and wish myself a Happy Birthday. I'm about to turn 28.

* * *

Exactly a week later, I find myself sitting, once more, in a musty, sweaty, makeshift holding cell – this time on the border of Togo and Benin. I am trying to explain to Togo's Head of Border Security why I'm here and why I was taking pictures of his precious *frontiere*.

It doesn't really make sense to me either. I happened to be near Togo for a meeting on a Friday afternoon in neighboring Ghana and am cursed by a lengthy bucket list ever-burning a hole in my metaphysical pocket.

There wasn't anything in particular I wanted to see in Togo. But I had never biked across an African country before. Why I wanted this particular experience this particular weekend, I cannot quite explain. Nonetheless, at 32 miles wide, Togo seemed like the right choice for such a meaningless, arbitrary goal, and I was with two work friends who were also convinced of the merits of such an undertaking.

We arrived in the country, bought crappy bikes from a local market, and prepared for our journey. Early the next morning, we set out with the coastal wind blowing in our faces – passing groups of runners, fishermen heading out to sea, and a large number of people carrying things on their heads.

Within two hours, it was all over. We triumphantly leaned our bikes against the "Frontiere Benin e Togo" sign and began to document our conquest.

This was frowned upon and so, here we are.

The heavy-set man in front of us looks amused and not overly upset. Yet the glint in his eye reveals he is sizing up how he is going to come out ahead in this odd situation.

The rich-looking white humanitarian tourist-types in front of him don't have any money, so a bribe is out of the question. To be fair, our plan (as it were) was simply to ride the bikes back whence we came.

This explanation doesn't quite satisfy. He offers us cokes, then wants to hear more about our travels and what we were hoping to accomplish with our impetuous trip across his country.

After a while, it becomes clear that he is stalling, keeping us here until we offer him something.

We offer him the bikes in exchange for a ride back across the country. With a minimal amount of further posturing, he agrees, thus concluding one of the odder chapters of my journey.

An hour later we're back at our hotel celebrating and congratulating ourselves profusely. The next day, it's close, but we make it to the airport on time.

We are whisked – safely and more or less in comfort – back to our strange world at the "pinnacle" where it's more normal for people like us to have too much time and money on our hands with which to bizarrely demonstrate, with our tales from the road, how adventurous, and spontaneous, and unique, and interesting, and enviable we are amidst a drab sea of nameless others.

Chapter 39

There's a race of men that don't fit in,
A race that can't stay still;
So they break the hearts of kith and kin,
And they roam the world at will.
They range the field and they rove the flood,
And they climb the mountain's crest;
Theirs is the curse of the gypsy blood,
And they don't know how to rest.
Robert W. Service

Those weeks romping around West Africa with good work friends yielded perhaps the highest concentration of stories from my work travel, but they were by no means unique in the nature of the adventures.

In my full-time job at the lab, I was building and leading a team which advised international organizations and foreign government agencies on how to reach poor people more effectively and efficiently with aid money and social programming.

Whatever else you picture about such a job, you probably imagine (correctly) that it requires significant international travel.

Sometimes this travel was to speak with partners and make sure our project teams had what they needed to be successful. Occasionally, the travel was to attend a conference or event. Sometimes, frequently, these trips were to conduct field research – learning directly from the folks who actually live in these far-away places.

Regardless of the exact rationale, there was always a reason to be on the road. During my first five months – before I learned how to say no to this faucet hose-style exploration – I traveled to East Asia three times and West Africa twice. In nautical miles it was all the way around the circumference of the globe five times in as many months.

After waking from the inevitable jet-lag induced coma, I established some boundaries, and that pace softened somewhat – if not significantly – for the next three years.

Each place was not as inherently bizarre as Monrovia or the Togolese border with Benin. Nonetheless, every time I traveled for work some crazy adventure inevitably found me. At this point, it was in my blood.

* * *

During business trips over the next few years, I would ride motorcycles through remote islands in the Philippines; climb the tallest mountain in the South Pacific; race and win the Mt. Kilimanjaro Marathon in Tanzania; travel to the Fiji Water Plant in, yes, Fiji; and puke all over gorgeous Douro Valley Portugal after a night of bad paella.

For an otherworldly afternoon in Senegal, I'd walk the art colony which has emerged on Île d' Gorée. I'd reflect on the sad history of this westernmost patch of the continent where, for hundreds of years, millions of people left their homes in chains to literally build – against their will – the great nation from which I hail.

For an otherworldly morning in Colombia, I would count out and distribute $10,000 in cash to local businessmen – brought with me over the border to the cocaine capital of the world. Handling the payments on the glass table of my hotel room (for a workshop my team was hosting) was actually entirely legal and above-board. It also easily could've been a scene straight out of Narcos.

* * *

These stories of my travels at work rank as my favorites amongst the many others I will spare my reader but enjoy retelling to any who will listen.

Such bizarre, quirky, often unpleasant, frequently self-indulgent, but nonetheless intriguing stories from the road are what people think of when they envision a path like the one I've traveled. In many ways, they would be right in their assumptions. The continued, consistent presence of such tales – deep into my professional life – allowed crazy, spontaneous travel to burrow its way ever deeper into a superficial sense of who I was.

In another very real sense, small adventures such as these served merely as asides to the story of a very full life for me during those years.

* * *

Alongside the extensive work travel and challenging full-time job, I had also stayed on as a consultant at my previous employer, a board member at Willy's growing NGO in Uganda, and was training diligently for my new favorite missed-opportunity-washed-up-athlete-proving-ground: IronMan Triathlons.

Over those years at the lab, I grew to enjoy the challenge of executing more than seemed humanly possible. This too was becoming part of what I saw as core to who I was.

I thrived on the frequent movement and the constant challenge. I was forever striving, improving, and demonstrating competence and was working on all fronts at what I felt was the exact intersection of my abilities and interests – I had created this identity for myself.

Alas, more than merely "enjoy" the challenge and change and new experience, I ultimately found I needed it.

When, at long last, I stopped working two jobs and stepped back from my role on Willy's board and cut back on my swim, bike, and run mileage, I found I was still missing something.

The fullness and busyness of my life had masked a deep anxiety; I lacked a knowledge and awareness of what I really needed to be doing and who I really needed to be.

* * *

We'd lived in our new hometown for three years, but it still felt transient, temporary. The thought of really setting down roots in this place was never something I could quite get my head around.

I was committed to being there for Rachel's education. Yet, the idea that it might be the best thing for me, for us, to stay a while longer never stuck.

It wasn't that I didn't enjoy my existence in this picturesque town. In fact, our quality of life was ideal. We rented a townhouse on the same block as my office, with a five-minute walk for Rachel. There were fun things to do in town, some interesting people, and beautiful places to exercise or rest nearby. It was from this charmed vantage point that I "endured" my time supporting Rachel's journey through grad school.

Nonetheless, as the side gigs and crazy hours of training gradually faded away, all I could think about was the next thing. We'd always talked about going back overseas to live, and the allure of a life of travel with Rachel beckoned.

When Rachel finally finished up school, we would have our moment.

It probably would've been better for her to work in her field. It certainly would've been better for me to invest deeply in the seeds of community and rootedness we'd planted and watered those last three years.

But, when Rachel finally finished up school, we would have our moment.

I was teaching a two-week course in Cuba and leading

a project along the Colombia-Venezuela border, so I had somewhat of a work excuse to hit the road. I made the case to our Director that it would be advantageous to my team if I spent the next year working from the region. It wasn't her first choice, but she graciously agreed.

Rachel also agreed and when she finally finished up school, we had our moment.

Three days after her graduation, our stuff was back in storage and we were heading south.

Chapter 40

True consciousness is not so much about awareness as it is skill, that is, the ability to place our action within an intelligible narrative.
Stanley Hauerwas, The Ethics of Character

Heading south would start with a month in idyllic Puebla, Mexico, brushing up on our Spanish before continuing our journey. Puebla is a beautiful high-altitude city in Central Mexico with a thriving middle class and a general resilience to the violence which has plagued most of the country these last decades.

My job and our personal travels would eventually take us south through Cuba, Costa Rica, Panama, Colombia, Venezuela, Uruguay, Argentina, and Chile, then back up through Bolivia and Peru over the next six months.

Our Spanish was sufficient to survive this journey, but not to thrive in it and certainly not to function in a business setting.

We found a terrific immersive language program with small classes and a kind host family. In other words, this was an ideal situation for language learning with strong incentives to engage fully.

One problem though.

* * *

I want to be fluent in Spanish, but I don't want to learn, not really anyway.

Something deep within me resists being taught or corrected or subjected to the instruction of another. I don't want to study or be challenged or have setbacks. I find myself bucking, tensing when corrected, and despondent when progress stalls.

Yet growth cannot come apart from these struggles. I will never achieve my goals in this space or in others if I find myself unwilling to fail, to be pushed by another – to be formed.

I was given the option to engage in this course of study during the coming months and, indeed, I chose to do so.

I chose.

Is not such a choice the epitome of freedom as our society defines it?

* * *

Ultimately, choice is and can be only part – a small part, in fact – of freedom. Whatever freedom I truly possess will express itself through my ability to act *rightly* against my individual whims and cravings, be driven toward other choices worth making, and continue choosing *rightly*.

So how do I manifest this freedom in my life today? What is demanded of me in order to choose *rightly* and thus be free from the bondage of my own weak, selfish desires?

At a high level, I'd posit that the answer to the above is a simple: I need strong character. That word "character," however, carries certain connotations in American and, particularly, American Christian society from which I want to distance my intent.

I'm not talking about character in the sense of my having an arbitrary, universal obligation to follow certain rules (known as deontological ethics). Nor am I suggesting you might somehow be able to quantifiably measure my character today by the consequences of a particular act or set of actions (known as utilitarian ethics).

Rather, character – that thing which can allow us to be truly free – is the authentic embodiment, the fulfillment of a series of practices which can only be developed within specific communities and traditions with particular histories.

So, that sounds good in theory, right? Or maybe it doesn't. But what does "true character being best developed within specific communities" actually look like? And, what does *rightly* even mean?

* * *

Back to my Spanish language struggles. Language learning is a fantastic exemplar of community's role in character development and what it means to be *right*. Alone as an individual, you will fail. You may teach yourself lots of grammar and vocab and speak whatever language emerges from your individual studying, but it will not be aligned with the needs of a community. It will not serve a purpose greater than personal enrichment. It won't be *right* in the sense that it won't really be Spanish.

Ultimately, in this scenario, I will be alone with my learning. Whatever crazy rules I create for myself to follow can just as easily be broken when my mood shifts (or when things get tough).

However, with a community to support me, I have grounding. I can be encouraged by others, formed by their understanding of the language and culture. I can proceed with confidence.

I can know with certainty this is the *right* way because lots of other folks are formed *rightly* by this community – i.e., they all understand each other and have for hundreds and hundreds of years.

With a community behind me, it's not that I am entitled to go around boasting how I have all the answers and insisting everyone should speak just like me. Rather, to the extent I learn to live (as well as speak, read, write, and listen in this case) within the bounds of the rules set by this community, I can know that the way I am living is *true*.

As I sat there in that empty classroom considering this line of reasoning, the real question slowly came into focus: *where is my community?*

* * *

We each have many such communities which help us define our identities and speak the specific language of citizen, employee, parent, friend, whatever.

For me, I found my identity as a husband and a Christian, but also as a spontaneous traveler, a leader, someone with entertaining stories, a humanitarian of sorts, and an endurance athlete, even if only of middling success.

There is nothing inherently wrong with these varying identities or their specific dialects. Yet, you can't expect to speak multiple languages coherently at the same time, can you?

In order to live authentically, to live in truth, to avoid despondency when life and failure inevitably collide with our competing identities, we have to somehow prioritize. We have to choose which community, which identity, which language is most important to us. We have to know which will actually give us the power to speak and live coherently in this life while preparing us for the next.

Once we've made that decision, "character development" becomes the task of diving deeply into what it means to live coherently as a member of that community, rejecting those rules and practices which do not belong to that tradition and embracing more fully those which do.

* * *

Don't get me wrong. Mine is not a self-help story. Making such a commitment to a single community – particularly an *authentically* Christian one – will place you immediately at odds with your other communities and the competing identities they would see you espouse.

For this very reason, late-modern western culture has evolved to teach us to hold our beliefs, communities, relationships, our very identities loosely, to break free from the bonds of our particular circumstances, and to embrace limitless choice as an individual being.

But, in a world where you, the individual, are the only one with an opinion which matters, where does your meaning come from? Who are you anyway? What language are you speaking?

* * *

I was increasingly recognizing a clash, an incongruence between my identities as a "global citizen" and "digital nomad" and the lessons I felt I'd been learning – intellectually at least – about the value of community and place.

A life committed to community and deep relationship in Puebla, or London, or rural Northern Myanmar is certainly no worse than one in DC, or Denver, or rural Virginia. Each community poses its own challenges – perhaps even more so internationally – but embracing and empathizing with challenge is what close relationship is all about.

Yet, there is a stark difference between a life committed to *a* place and *a* people – foreign or domestic – and a life of disconnected sampling, testing, exploration.

In this moment, this empty classroom, I found myself decidedly on the latter path. And for these next several months, this was the path I had committed to follow. There was still much to gain on this journey, but a realization of the emptiness and destructiveness of the life I'd sought, pursued, and attained slowly began to sink in.

Chapter 41

The secret to change is to focus all of your energy, not on fighting the old, but on building the new.
Socrates

As we approached Cuba's northern shore in the throes of heavy turbulence and I gained sight of the rugged, misty coastline, I was overwhelmed with inspiration by the beauty of the novel landscape and the intense battle for meaning and significance playing out in my soul.

In this long-awaited moment, at the start of a new adventure out on the open road, I found myself equal parts grateful and distressed, excited and forlorn, engaged and cynical. Reflecting on these mixed emotions in flight, I scribbled furiously into my notepad.

Haunted by the wind-tossed rolling waves, the cerulean depths, the deep, lush foreboding jungled reaches of this new land and my own troubled soul; I long for adventure and newness and dislocation and detachment. In the same breath, I know I need the patchwork quilt of community's broken, hurting, hurtful embrace to wrap me away from my piercing aloneness.

Both paths and the combination of the two excite and terrify as life (and this plane) struggles, writhes, lurches forward, onward, downward into the heart of this short existence.

* * *

A land of contradictions, Cuba is an eclectic mix and a cohesive unit all its own – a flawless complement to my (clearly raging) internal turmoil.

In some ways, Havana is perhaps the most beautiful and perfect travel destination I've ever visited. It is safe, aesthetically pleasing, politically and culturally distinct, historically compelling, and palpably alive with energy.

In other ways, it epitomizes my nagging concerns with the impact of a western worldview – our posture toward growth and "freedom" and the beck and call of the open road – on our souls and the people and places we encounter.

In the face of evermore open ideas and open markets and open borders the existing society cannot stand.

The tide of ideas, opportunities, and allure of individual liberty will prove too much for the authoritarian socialist system which is already quaking under the weight of its own insufficiencies. Indeed, the cracks are already as visible as those in the walls around us in Old Havana.

Yet, without the current system of government, the strongpoints of this society – the relative equality, the free education, the stellar health care, the distinct culture and the sense of community – will fall as well.

While visibly and explicitly serving an oppressive function, the government also serves a quiet, implicit, but no less real protective function against the destructive, dislocating, disorienting forces brought by the mirage of infinite choice, liberty, and happiness. That this mirage so fully captivates the minds and imagination of our society – of me personally – is a testament to our own blindness and foolishness in attempting to cast judgment on these people, their system.

* * *

A few short weeks later the course is over, and I leave this country, once again inspired, but alas, unchanged. Still "fighting the old," as Socrates said, yet unsure exactly how to "build the new." Still excited for the next adventure, hoping it will tell me something new about myself. Still confused and distraught by the weight of my individual moral failings. Still fleeing commitments and rootedness with all my might. Still.

Yet I also leave deeply grateful for the opportunity to explore this place frozen in time, for employment at a university which values exposing students to the mystery of life beyond our borders, and for a life full of people and experiences able to speak truth into my life even if I'm not quite brave enough to act on that truth.

* * *

In the next month, we traveled through the cloud forests and jungled coastlines of Costa Rica and Panama before settling in misty, mountainous Bogotá, Colombia.

Perhaps settling is the wrong word. We paused for a moment and spent more than a few days or weeks in this place. We stayed at a friend's apartment for the next three months while I worked from the city to get a project off the ground.

We made friends with her friends and attended her church and learned the rhythms of daily Bogotaño life. We found the markets and chose a favorite bakery and learned to hate waiting in lines at Colombian grocery stores.

But this approximation of normalcy in Bogotá was just that. There was always a fixed end date in sight, and we were confronted daily with the sheer impossibility of "laying down roots" somewhere in a matter of months.

Sure, I was working, but in the end, we were still tourists. We were there to experience and collect pictures and hope that these moments in a foreign city might somehow make us more than what we were when we arrived.

* * *

Beyond what our extended stay in Colombia reminded us about ourselves, we were also reminded that the broader nomadic lifestyle trend impacts lives abroad in ways often unseen amidst the Instagram storylines.

Nowhere were these hidden impacts more apparent to us than in La Guajira. South America's remote, northern-most desert peninsula is rapidly becoming a tourist hotspot given its austere, otherworldly landscapes and unique indigenous culture.

Rachel artfully encapsulated our thoughts on the region in an article she published in a travel magazine a few weeks later.

The dry wind sweeps desert dirt and endless trash across long and lonely miles, twisting around cacti and through *yotojoro* huts. Barefoot children sit alongside dusty roads. Days are spent waiting in hammocks or squatting by the road, looking for the benevolent visitor in a big 4×4 coming from another world. Tourism shapes the culture just as the incessant wind shapes and shifts the landscape...

Bootlegged Venezuelan gas in reused soda bottles hung from roadside stands, strengthening the Wayuu's ties to – and exploitation by – organized crime networks, but making it easier for the traveler to venture deeper into the Colombian outback. Ancestral lands were now the backdrop for social media photo shoots. Traditions and cultural rituals morphed into consumable, on-demand performances for curious visitors.

And yet, we saw tourism bringing much-needed money to the region. The beautiful, woven Wayuu mochila bag is generating income for Wayuu women and becoming a hot new trend for spenders beyond the desert. Adventure tourism brings money to select Wayuu hotels as well as to clans that open their homes to indigenous tourism, educating outsiders on dress, dance, and culture.

But I wonder how much benefit our presence brings to the outstretched hands of Wayuu children; how much our

money betters these lives. Tourism's myriad moral merits and drawbacks are too complex to fully decipher. Yet, one thing is certain: in a powerful way it shifts the landscape, like the dry wind shapes the land.
(Rachel Sims, *The Stranger's Guide*, 2018)

* * *

Guajira is not alone as a shifting landscape. A mounting tidal wave of selfie-centric tourism was preparing to descend on Colombia.

At the time of our trip (2018), there were still places considered *fuerte* or "dangerous due to active guerrilla conflict" by the locals. Nevertheless, Colombia was becoming daily more secure for the savvy traveler interested in veering off the beaten path. Sure, Cartagena is beautiful, but the fact that 75% of Colombia's 2018 international tourists only made it that far is baffling.

Colombia's coffee region – Eje Cafetero – with its 200ft tall wax palm forests, sweeping valleys, snow-capped mountains, and flawless climate – stands as one of my top five favorite destinations globally.

Boyaca – with its stunning small towns, other-worldly *paramo*, and perfectly banked curving country roads – isn't far behind.

And these name just a few. Cali is supposed to be one of the world's great cities; Tyronna, one of its best beaches; Riticuba Blanca one of the Andes most magnificent mountains; oh, and then there's the Amazon.

It really hit home for me, though, in Medellín, where we were celebrating our anniversary.

The 1999 murder capital of the world may not come to mind as an ideal, romantic getaway, but the winds of change are as visible here as anywhere else in the country. This is truly a city on the rise.

Medellín for us was defined by its natural beauty, flawless weather, varied and tasty cuisine, lovely people, and sheer excitement to see tourists.

We took a free walking tour, ate delicious pizza, rode all over town on one of South America's few metros, and took a cable car out to a scenic park high above the city.

It was encouraging and beautiful to experience this resurgent city and its lovely Paisa people who were so visibly, vocally excited to see tourists finally returning after many years of tragedy and violence.

Yet, as in la Guajira, it was confusing and disturbing to see the onslaught of "TripAdvisor inequality."

During our days in Medellín and after, I became increasingly bothered by the phenomenon whereby certain places in town – specifically the ones catering to western, hipster tastes and style – become hugely successful on the basis of online reviews from tourists with money.

Even in a thriving resurgent locale like Medellín, other, more local places that don't fit this bill struggle and fail right next door.

You might say this is just survival of the fittest in a market economy. And you would be right.

But the depravity, the deep-seated mean streak at play in this system we take for granted as it props up our wealthy lives, really hit me in Medellín. I observed here, as elsewhere, monolithic "Western" society dominating smaller communities – a far-away culture with money is able to consume a local one, which remains marginal.

The trend offers a paradox. On one hand, a larger number of international tourists (and their money) are lured to the city by the promise that things won't be so different. They will certainly find a little taste of home in an exotic locale and as such are more willing to come.

This "luring" is economically good for the local people; at

least for the ones able to capitalize on global, affluent, viral trends by – for example – outfitting their "farm to table" venue with exposed wood beams and vintage artwork and long strings of incandescent light bulbs.

I suppose it is also good for the generation of tourists seeking something resembling a Mumford and Sons music video at every meal.

Less good for the local folk is how TripAdvisor inequality incentivizes abandonment of unique, authentic culture in pursuit of Instagram-friendly facades serving globalized cuisine – rendering hotspots in Medellín, Chiang Mai, and Addis indistinguishable in many ways from those in San Fran, Portland, and Amsterdam.

Those who refuse (or simply can't afford) to play the "mono-culture" game are left behind.

I'd love to say TripAdvisor inequality bothered me most because of my deep and abiding concern for the poor being crushed daily by the onslaught of a global marketplace. And that is a part of it for sure.

But the real truth is, when the time came to leave, Colombia had stolen our hearts, and it hurts me to think it might look very different if ever I am to return.

We could've stayed much longer and part of me wishes we had. But, alas, that wasn't the point of this trip. We had much more to see. And so, we journeyed south.

Chapter 42

*All paths lead to the same goal: to convey to others what we are.
And we must pass through solitude and difficulty, isolation and
silence in order to reach forth to the enchanted place where we can
dance our clumsy dance and sing our sorrowful song.*
Pablo Neruda

We first noticed my phone (and attached wallet) missing as
we started the hike; attempting a speedy 7-mile leg in the last,
fading hours of sun in order to arrive at our campsite before
dark. At this moment, streaking across the epic bottom of the
world, we came to realize that our earthly possessions had
become scattered across at least 13 different locations and two
continents, as we'd left little piles here and there for many
months on our journey south.

There were bags in southern Virginia, a storage unit outside
DC, a suitcase in Ohio, a few final items left at a friend's house in
Pennsylvania, a slew of books sent back to Oregon with friends
who visited us in Panama, Rachel's engagement ring safely with
my parents in Colorado, a suitcase of souvenirs in Bogotá, a
backpack at a hotel in Santiago and another in Puerto Natales,
amongst several others.

And then there was my phone, driver's license, and credit
card left on AutoBus Gomez #1354 flying down some Patagonian
backroad. Oh yeah, and us and our hiking boots and a small
pack on mile 2.1 of 53 of the most beautiful hike of our lives.

But these are just the physical things – as to the intangible
little piles of feelings, experiences, and memories we'd both left
and collected from the places we travel, it is impossible to say.

* * *

For the three months following Colombia, we had made no effort to approximate stability. We were on the road. No, not like in Puebla where we stayed with a host family for a month, not like Bogotá where we stayed in a friend's flat for three. This time we were really on the road.

We'd taken a disorienting red-eye flight to Buenos Aires and woke up thinking we were in a European city – except for the Latin American prices. I ran a marathon (continent #5) and attended a work conference (continent #6). We ate the best empanadas in the world and enjoyed excellent Italian food for the first time in months.

We passed briefly into Uruguay, but just for a day. The posh, coastal village of Colonia del Sacramento still felt like Europe, but most assuredly at European prices.

We bused overnight to Mendoza, the Napa Valley of the Southern hemisphere, and had the best Malbec of our lives.

We drove in a delirious, oxygen deprived haze to the base camp of Aconcagua and hiked far enough to see the highest peak in the world beyond the Himalayas.

Another four hours down the road and we found ourselves in Neruda's ambling, eclectic coastal hometown of Valparaiso, Chile. From "Valpo" we ambled gradually south through Chile – lingering in the bucolic wine country and the picturesque island of Chiloe with its cool, coastal walks and penguins and wool markets.

And then, we ventured south once more.

To reach our trailhead in *Parque Nacional Torres del Paine* where my wallet went missing, we'd taken a flight and a bus, and then another smaller bus passing *huanaco* and ostrich in the hills next to the road, and finally a ferry across a glacier blue lake to the starting point of our long trek through Patagonia's crown jewel.

* * *

Scattered, frantic, unrooted lives aside, Torres del Paine was otherworldly. As in, you truly felt you were on a different planet. Or perhaps Narnia, or Heaven.

On another trip, in the midst of a breathtaking 11-day hike through the heart of Switzerland, Rachel and I decided Europe's famous alps were a perfect 10 in terms of mountain beauty. Rocky Mountain National Park, Olympic National Park and Glacier National Park in the States are all strong 8s. The staggering yet austere heights atop the Andes and Himalayas get 9s in my book.

Torres del Paine is a 12.

In a spell of freakish good fortune, we had perfect weather, with sun, a little snow in a high mountain pass, and no wind. For four days, we saw nothing but glaciers, terrifying and beautiful mountains, and gray-blue lakes. We heard nothing but the streams and the birds and the sounds of ice and snow avalanches thundering across the valley.

And finally, after our last glorious mile, we recovered the first of our scattered possessions: my phone-wallet was miraculously turned in to the lovely rangers at the park service entrance.

Before we knew it, we were back on a plane to Santiago and then hurtling north on a whirlwind road trip from Chilean Atacama through Bolivia to Lima, Peru, and after another month on the road, the US of A, collecting little piles along the way.

* * *

Our natural human (or at least twenty-first-century American human) tendency is to glorify those areas in which we are different − if indeed we can identify any. This doesn't just apply to travel, but to decisions about where we live, how we vote (and why), where we work, when we achieved critical life benchmarks, what kind of car we drive, what kind of foods we like, etc.

Thus, it bears noting that our blissful blur of a journey through Latin America is, on one level, quite ordinary. There exist multiple guidebooks for every country: literal books telling you exactly what to do, where to stay, what to eat, how to get to *that* spot where you can take *that* picture.

TripAdvisor, Yelp, and Airbnb are as prolific here as anywhere in the States, millions of reviews all but eliminating the risk of a "bad experience." Improving infrastructure and cheap flights to practically everywhere complement these travel aids, dramatically reducing the difficulties, discomforts, and unknowns of long-term travel.

Dozens, if not hundreds, of Americans take trips of similar ambition through these lands each year. At least three have written comprehensive blogs authored to our exact demographic, documenting extensive, multi-year trips across the South American continent with a level of precision and style which makes feeling "off the beaten path" a bit of a farce.

Travel in the twenty-first century, with (all but) universal cellular data coverage, and a world of 2 billion other "wanderlust" millennials, is neither difficult nor extraordinary in any real sense. It is truly just a thing that some privileged people do.

However, within our circle of friends and family, amongst the "responsible class" of late 20 and early 30 something aspiring professionals pursuing a fairly standard, linear path, our journey represented a bit of an anomaly.

My point here is that we – while not exactly ye ole brave pioneers crossing the Andes on foot circa 1800 – were taking a different path for the moment.

And, it wasn't all penguins, mountains, and darling villages.

* * *

Beyond the mounting sense of disintegration and dislocation, travel is amazing. Travel with Rachel is even better than amazing. The ability to experience so many new places and people and food for such a long time with the person I love most in this life is a privilege which does not escape me, and one for which I am immensely grateful.

Yet, sometimes, travel is just completely and utterly un-glamorous. Every time you move to a different place you have to spend time unpacking and carefully re-packing your backpack. You have to buy the right amount of water to last until your next move, and you have to find new grocery stores and laundry facilities. Your sleep schedules get messed up, you eat way too many empanadas, and you don't exercise consistently. Sometimes you go way too long without washing your clothes; most of the time you look like a complete disaster.

* * *

So, yeah. It's not all lovely islands and penguins and wine tours out there on the open road. I mean, it is, but it is also getting testy with your partner on last-minute, late-night planning sprees, taking twice as long to do basic things because the internet sucks, and missing loved ones like crazy.

A journey is not about the highs, but how you handle the lows. And frankly, I don't handle them all that well.

Chapter 43

Travel isn't always pretty. It isn't always comfortable. Sometimes it hurts, it even breaks your heart. But that's okay. The journey changes you; it should change you. It leaves marks on your memory, on your consciousness, on your heart, and on your body. You take something with you. Hopefully, you leave something good behind.
Anthony Bourdain

It's well after midnight on some winding mountain pass in Southern Peru when I wake up from a dream trip to:

Kick, kick, kick. Pause. Kick, kick, kick. Throaty cough. Kick. Pause. Kick, kick.

This was my constant rhythm for our overnight journey from Northern Bolivia into Peru. At 10pm, after four hours on-board, the bus stopped in Puno and on came a group of 20 or 30 rambunctious locals, fresh off what must have been a rollicking time out on the town. She was amongst them, the one who would try my patience.

A journey is not about the highs, but how you handle the lows.

From the start, we were never going to be friends. I, near sleep with my seat reclined at the identical angle to every other passenger on the bus. She, wide awake, intoxicated, and indignant at my presumptuousness, interested in accepting neither my presence nor the angle of my chair.

A journey is not about the highs, but how you handle the lows.

For eight wearisome hours we battled. She, kicking, huffing, coughing on me and muttering mean things about me in Quechua. Me, clenching my fists, holding my ground, and thinking mean thoughts about her in a brain-jumbled mix of English and Spanish.

A journey is not about the highs, but how you handle the lows.

Finally, as the sun rose over Cusco, the least favorite bus ride of my life mercifully came to a close, and I was reminded for the thousandth time the most critical, difficult, and important lesson the road can teach you.

A journey is not about the highs, but how you handle the lows.

Frankly, I don't handle them all that well.

* * *

On this note, we began our time in the Incan Empire. Cusco (particularly the San Blas neighborhood and historic center) is a majestic city. Cobblestone streets, colonial architecture, Incan stonework everywhere, the Sacred Valley (home to famed Machu Picchu) just over the next ridge. It is, in many ways, the quintessential, lovely South American town.

Perhaps for this reason, it is decidedly, 100% infested and spilling over with tourists. We came in "low" season, which simply meant that the countless touts – hawking massages, artwork, trinkets, and drugs – were just that much more aggressive.

Cusco and the Sacred Valley were by far the most unapologetically touristy places I've encountered in my travels. They were also amongst the most lovely. Go figure.

* * *

It's hard to imagine being "blown away" by an image you've probably seen thousands of times throughout your life. However, for all the hype, for all the built-up expectations and off-putting touristic infrastructure, Machu Picchu did not disappoint.

We left our hotel at 4:30am for the steep 1.5 hour walk up to the park entrance.

At 6:00am, we entered the park in a wave of humanity, very glad to have purchased the extra "Machu Picchu mountain experience" which was only open to a few hundred people per day.

Around 8:30am, we made it to the top in a total cloud. We had little more than 200 feet of visibility during our first few hours in the park. However, after more than 4,500 ft of climbing, we received a stunning reward.

For over two hours, we watched in awe as the clouds lifted – first to reveal the surrounding mountains, then the valley, and finally the *coup de gras*.

Quietly, above all the noise; above the incessant self-marketing; above the dirty capitalism and corrupt special interests which keep prices to this natural, historical treasure sky high; above the thousands of other tourists here to check this thing off their damned list of must-visit tourist grinds; above the gritty, colonial debasement of the great culture to whom this place was once sacred; we had our moment. The Peruvian sun rising, softly melting away clouds over Machu Picchu, was one of the most inspiring and surreal vistas I've ever encountered. All the smuck and overcrowding and loud visitors and tourist extortion and existential angst in the world couldn't detract from the grandeur. And believe me, it tried.

We eventually sauntered down from our perch and walked the ruins with the masses. By 11:30 or so, the place had cleared out significantly, completing the serenity of our Machu Picchu experience. There was even a pack of extremely tame llamas roaming the ruins – better for Instagram than lawnmowers, I suppose. We made friends with them, and I took a little nap right in the heart of this once Sacred Valley.

* * *

We passed the next few days in the leafy, coastal Miraflores neighborhood of Lima. These days were all about strolls along the seawall and cheap, world-class ceviche, watching the parasailers and surfers, and preparing mentally for our imminent return to the States.

And then, just like that, Latin America was a wrap and a new journey awaited stateside. As we continued north – reclaiming our "piles of stuff" – we reflected on the places and people our hearts now longed to reclaim as well.

This journey was beautiful and difficult in all the ways you hope and imagine travel will be... and then some.

It was also a moment of imaginative fusion for me: of a long-held intellectual understanding to a deeply felt hope for the beauty and difficulty of a different kind of journey.

Chapter 44

I have come home at last! This is my real country! I belong here.
This is the land I have been looking for all my life, though I never
knew it till now... Come further up, come further in!
C.S. Lewis, The Last Battle

To be clear, if it is not already crystally so within these pages,
I do not consider myself fully transformed by the lessons I'm
learning along this winding path. A movement toward true
identity certainly begins with awareness, but really *learning*
is a journey which requires the kind of character only formed
through community.

Yet, I find my strange community of Christ-followers broken
and striving after substitutes and idols and false consciousness
the same as myself. They haven't lifted themselves out of their
own depravity, so how might they lift me?

* * *

As I reflect on this nagging question, I find myself transported
to the black stone beach of gray-blue Lago Nordenskjold in the
shadow of the mighty *Los Cuernos del Paine* in Chilean Patagonia.

This is, without question, the most spectacularly beautiful
place I've ever encountered.

We're a mile or so from our campsite and Rachel is hiking on,
but I am affixed, alone for a moment with my thoughts.

I sit here, rolling two glacier-smoothed pebbles in my palm
and pondering this very question of how a broken community
of believers could possibly be the arms to lift me from my own
brokenness.

I consider our common existential struggle, our desperate
clinging and striving for transcendence, for experiences and

things we hope will elevate and define our lives – and the utter universality of this selfish, futile struggle.

I think also of the moments of beauty and wholeness we stumble upon when we aren't even looking.

I think of Bill – who, before he even knew he was doing so, held my head above water as I struggled to recognize the hint of a plan for my life, held in store by a God who cares.

I think of Ben – who, after just a brief meeting, welcomed me into his home and started a lifelong friendship with a dumb American kid just looking for a cheap London room.

I think of my parents who made a brave decision at the height of a career which inspired in me a deep questioning of, if not quite escape from, a life in pursuit of material gain.

I think, most of all, of my closest confidants at the various stages of my journey: of my sister during childhood, Jeremy as I began to find myself as a young adult, and Rachel with whom I daily share my walk.

These, amongst countless others – though they were still seeking the character necessary to become the people they were created to be – loved me unconditionally and in so doing, spoke truth into my life, encouraging me in my most challenging moments and significant decisions.

I think now of Jeremy's young son, Jack, and the smooth stones I hold in my hands, insufficient gifts found here at the bottom of the world.

These gifts were born of one last story which began years earlier. I know not what good they will ultimately serve, merely that they must be given.

* * *

While I was living in Thailand almost a decade earlier, Jeremy sent me an email asking for a favor and gift of sorts. He wanted me to "pick up some clothes he'd left at the dry cleaner" when he was living in the same city... 8 months prior!

I thought he was messing with me, but he sent me directions, so I went to the store. Surprise of surprises, his clothes were still there. True to form, the owner immediately recognized me (as Jeremy) and rushed over to give me the bag of clean clothes, scolding me a little for leaving them so long.

It was another six months before I returned them to their rightful owner. When I did, Jeremy informed me that – by way of a thank you – he had left a gift for me in another city.

"Paris," he said. "On the top floor of the Westin Vendôme. Go up the elevator. Turn left at the end of the hall and walk all the way to the corner facing the river. Open the window, climb out on the roof, and reach under the gutter. Feel for a ball of duct tape. Use what's inside on a nice dinner and consider it payment in full."

Amused and a bit confused, I replied, "Jeremy, that's awesome, but I'm not going to Paris."

"Oh, yes you are," he said with a smile. "Someday you are going to fall in love and marry the perfect girl and you're going to take her there."

And so, I did. Not two years later (and not without Jeremy's encouragement to embrace those "heights and depths"), I married Rachel. Another nine months after that, we were in Paris.

Alas, our time and budget were short, and I didn't make it to the roof-top that visit.

Then, eight years later, we had another opportunity. And what was the first thing I did when I got through security at Charles de Gaulle?

"Taxi to the Westin Vendôme, monsieur!"

I went through his paces and sure enough, leaning out over the courtyard, my fingers closed tightly around the corroded duct tape ball, and I pulled it free. A gift from Jeremy, almost a decade in the making.

Sitting against the wall in that quiet, luxurious hallway with a decade-old gift in my hands, I finally broke down. I knew I couldn't use it. After all that had transpired, it just didn't feel right. The gift isn't for me anymore. It's for Jack.

A week later, I re-hid the gift in another unlikely location in another of the great European cities.

Someday when he's ready, I'll give him the new directions. Or maybe we'll go find it together.

* * *

I smile at the memory, but looking up at the otherworldly crags of *Los Cuernos*, my heart grows heavy.

"Heights and depths," right? Mountains are always such a poignant reminder of that posture toward love and life Jeremy commended all those years ago; a posture clearly reflected in the story he told with his days.

I gaze 10,000 feet up into the heights of these majestic peaks and think back to my last trip out to beautiful Colorado.

He died in a climbing accident on Capitol Peak, an accomplished mountaineer and one of my dearest friends.

Few mountains have inspired my adventurous spirit more than the one right in front of me, and few humans more than Jeremy. Beyond a friend, Jeremy was a mentor, a confidant, a spiritual guide, a brother to me throughout this decade of oh-so non-linear personal growth.

With the exception of Rachel, no one knew me better or pushed me harder to become the best version of myself.

This loss is the saddest and most disorienting of my life. But, greater than my own loss or that of the countless lives he touched, I grieve here, on this most beautiful of beaches, for Jamie and Jack. There was nothing in this life Jeremy loved more than his wife and young son.

Like me, Jeremy wasn't perfect. He hadn't figured it all out.

He wrestled deeply with the distracting, corrupting seductions of a world which offers insufficient substitutes for identity. He sought adventure and excitement and exploration as ways to differentiate and find himself even though he knew in his heart they would never fulfill.

Yet in his life, Jeremy valued caring for others, particularly those in immense pain. His work combatting poverty and human trafficking overseas and, later, helping people struggling with addiction as a clinical therapist was an outpouring of his overall posture toward people in the midst of suffering.

And he cared for people in smaller ways. His gifts, his love, was meaningful, lasting, and authentic not in spite of his wrestle with his own brokenness, but because of it.

* * *

As I stand and walk away from this beach, this assured high-point in a life guaranteed of many lows, I am inspired and hopeful, if not quite at peace with how to approach the impossible task before me in the years, months, days, or hours I have left.

I cannot take with me the pure transcendence of this moment, the full grandeur and beauty and fullness I feel from such heights. This is not the kind of gift I can bring back for Jack or the countless other lives I will cross paths with who, like me, find themselves irreparably broken and damaged by the brutal course of life's depths.

What I do take with me are these two stones, themselves beaten, tossed, and hewn imperfect from the road they've traveled. These are for Jack, and I can't know fully what they will mean for him or how my broken gestures attempting love might influence his life or others.

In this unknowing and only in it, can I take and offer the hope and courage which comes from having lived a little and messed up a lot and realized that such a hope comes from a lost and wandering place unseen and never fully knowable.

For only in a persisting willingness to stumble and strive and humbly journey *together* might we catch a glimpse of the love of the One who made us; He who beckons us "further up and further in" toward true union with one another and Himself in the more perfect life which surely awaits beyond all this.

Conclusion

The man with the clear head is the man who... looks life in the face, realizes that everything in it is problematic, and feels himself lost. And this is the simple truth — that to live is to feel oneself lost — he who accepts it has already begun to find himself, to be on firm ground. Instinctively, as do the shipwrecked, he will look round for something to which to cling, and that tragic, ruthless glance, absolutely sincere, because it is a question of his salvation, will begin to bring order into the chaos of his life. These are the only genuine ideas; the ideas of the shipwrecked. All the rest is rhetoric, posturing, farce. He who does not really feel himself lost, is without remission; that is to say, he never finds himself, never comes up against reality.

Jose Ortega y Gasset, The Revolt of the Masses

It was always more than escape and medication that I sought in those moments with the wind blowing in my face. It was identity and significance. It was an ultimate meaning, the kind of absolute, universal certainty not fully available in this life. In essence, it was a grasping, as Ortega says, "to be on firm ground."

For me and perhaps many others at the *pinnacle*, our wander-lost hearts seem ever bent in desperate search for something we will not find. Even as the waves threaten to consume us, we fail to recognize that we are, inescapably, shipwrecked in an unjust world of our own collective making.

Faced with such a problematic, dangerous, uncertain world, our lives too often tell the story of a clinging to the natural, human tendency for *belief*, over the far more un-natural (rather, supernatural), but transformative response of surrendering in *faith*.

Somewhere along the way, we have gotten terribly lost

219

regarding the definitions of these terms and all they imply for our shipwrecked lives. And, as French sociologist and lay theologian Jacques Ellul quite poignantly states, "We have an annoying tendency to confuse the two."

I submit that the distinction is critical for understanding the roots of millennial wanderlust, niche connoisseurship, our clamoring pursuit of immortality, and our quixotic flight from the inevitability of death. As such, I suspect that a deep, soul-level embrace of the distinction is key for my own – and perhaps others' – spiritual survival amidst the various idols of this terrible, beautiful shipwreck we call the present.

On one hand, beliefs are the necessary building blocks for existence and thriving as humans. We build our beliefs largely (but not fully) on the basis of rationality and empirical observation. In other words, we believe what our senses tell us to be true about the world.

We tend to believe things we perceive as proven through experience: that (usually) buildings won't spontaneously crumble when we go to the second floor; that our neighbor (likely) won't stab us when we walk over to ask about his week; that (generally), cars drive on the left in the UK and its former colonial dominion and on the right in the rest of the world. We (well, some of us) believe scientific findings and formulas because they've been proven in empirical studies many times over and because they produce a consistent result upon which we can rely.

Beliefs are those tools with which we construct our natural lives, the things we take for granted from observation and experience. As creatures who crave certainty, we like our beliefs since they help us derive an illusion of "firm ground" from our existence amidst the rolling, endless sea of life.

Critically, beliefs are also what bind us together as communities and societies. Without a minimum of shared beliefs, a society cannot exist and will soon dissolve. We are thus encouraged by our society to hold and form and fight for our beliefs – and ultimately to be governed by the beliefs deemed most "reasonable" or "useful" by those in power.

Beliefs can also be spiritualized. Given the human (and easily politicized) nature of beliefs, we all too frequently seek – or are offered without asking – human, political means to enforce them.

This is where we run into trouble.

As Christians, we believe what the Bible says about how Christians should behave sexually and therefore use politics in an attempt to coerce non-Christians into alignment with this belief. We believe in peace, so we offer our support to a government which kills in peace's name. We are overcome by the insignificance and conformity of our fleeting lives, so we deify our individuality and believe that our rootless materialism will save us from the tragic superficiality of our souls.

Faith is different. It doesn't ask us to use our rationality to create a solution to a problem. Faith is hope in those things unseen and unknown.

In our hyper-individualized, hyper-rationalized version of Christianity, we all too often forget that God is and must be ultimately unknowable, unresolvable, in order to be worth our faith in the first place.

God is not merely the abstract projection of our own desires, aspirations, or values – even though we often treat Him this way. If He were, He wouldn't be God at all, but just another of our own creations which aid us in the development of productive societies.

Nor is God fully knowable. We can know pieces of His character, but the true nature of His justice, His mercy, His peace, His love, are complex and mysterious and powerful beyond our ability to fully grasp.

Rather, God is, as Ellul characterizes Him, "fundamentally other" "inevitably different from what pagans call God" and

221

thus, "unable to be fully assimilated into a system of belief." For, again, beliefs are based on things we have *fully* identified and defined and, through this definition, determined a rational approach for action.

If beliefs are productive, useful for society, and easily actionable, then faith is the opposite. Faith is a disturbing force which asks us to release our imagined control over outcomes to an unknowable God who descends upon us.

Faith is hope. And, as Ellul again suggests, "a hope founded in realism."

The realism is expressed when we accept the inevitability of suffering; that human existence is tragic and broken and unredeemable on its own.

The hope flows from faith in a force: a God beyond our comprehension – beyond rational proof – who desires union with us and through His freely offered love, redeems us who are broken beyond redemption.

Without grounding in this sort of unbelievable faith, human existence – including a supposedly Christian existence – is based on nothing more than false consciousness and deluded ideology.

But if we base our faith in the only realistic hope for humanity's redemption – a God beyond our comprehension who loves us beyond our ability to receive or deserve it – we can start afresh the humble, courageous journey as travelers in the greater adventure of His glory instead of our own.

Perhaps then, we will confront the sin we see in the world with prayer and repentance for our own complicity instead of attempting to coerce a secular world to accept "Christian" policy agendas.

Perhaps then, we will choose, in spite of the risk to our own safety, to stand in love with those who face violence and persecution instead of supporting at arm's length a government which seeks to abolish death via more death.

Perhaps then, we will confront the emptiness of late-modern consumerism not by a re-tooling and re-prioritization of which things (or experiences) we let define us, but by a rejection of possessions and human experience as a means by which to measure our lives.

Perhaps then, we will begin to find ourselves on firm ground as we learn what it truly means to live by faith: a "confidence in what we hope for and assurance about what we cannot see" (Hebrews 11:1).

Epilogue

Why not be utterly changed into fire?
Apophthegmata Patrum

In the end, we collected all those piles, returned to America, bought a house in that picturesque college town and prepared to part ways with a life of movement.

Shortly thereafter, I penned the SFD or "shitty first draft" – as Anne Lamott so aptly calls them – of this manuscript. Still writhing against full awareness of my own limited perspective, I believed my SFD to be a mature treatise against the hollow, destructive tendencies of our age not to mention an airtight personal alibi in the event of my slipping forever into bourgeois suburban malaise.

Then, on October 22, 2019, I received a message chalk full of wisdom from my dear friend pseudonymousDan (pDan). The implications of pDan's email blew up these assumptions and deeply informed the editing process.

More importantly, his insights tell the story of the unexpected journey Rachel and I began walking during the 2.5 years between SFD and today as I send *WanderLOST* off to press in early 2022.

pDan: It's here. Decision time. And not one decision, but a myriad of interwoven decisions that seemingly all have an effect on one another. Furthermore, there exists a sense of inevitability about this opportunity and all it "means". "Surely, this is where Jake's passions have led him," we might say to ourselves. But there is less "Jake" today than there once was; today there is a greater, more mysterious entity known as "Jake y Rachel," the two becoming one on a journey together that is better than the sum of its parts. Therefore this decision cannot merely be for the advancement of one, but the whole. Together, you operate out of a position of strength and passion to be broken vessels for this world, each bringing their extraordinary skills and depths to the great tasks before them. It is beautiful.

The "decision" in question was whether to accept an offer of employment which would take us across the world for several years to lead International Justice Mission's work in Cambodia. In that moment, we longed deeply for constancy and rootedness and rest in our comfortable new lives as stateside homeowners. Needless to say, such a significant move was not in line with "the plan."

Yet, we also knew that deep ties can be formed in Southeast Asia the same as in Southeast Virginia. Good opportunities existed on the horizon for Rachel in Phnom Penh and a return to IJM in such a capacity appeared to be truly a full circle moment for me.

But wait. Here's the kicker...

pDan: With that in mind it is no surprise to me that you desire to bring children into a life so oriented by love. While I'm of course proud and excited for all Rachel does with her extraordinary talents as a therapist (and I am always proud and excited for Jake and whatever it is that he does), I'm even more proud and excited you (both) would be brave enough to "choose" to bring children into your journey. It is good. It is fashionable it seems to pontificate about the wisdom of bringing children into a warming, violent, and undoubtedly fallen world. It is not a new concern. Choosing to have a child in a world that is warming, violent, and fallen is sometimes, however, a "simple" testimony of hope (think Ellul's brand of faith!). It is good.

Yes, you read that correctly. After a literal book of reflections on the inanity of travel and its destructive force on my life and the world, I was contemplating bringing a (yet theoretical) infant to an impoverished, authoritarian country just months before the biggest global travel lockdown in history.

pDan: Family matters, of course. In our late-modern American Christian culture we have no doubt what that means, while great doubt is surely due. The earliest Christians literally baptized their children unto death. Their witness haunts our sanitized account of "family values." Thankfully, and I mean that wholeheartedly, we do not live in such times, nor in such a place. But it's a counterweight to our cultural notions, no matter how *"Christian"* they are purported to be.

So many of our external pursuits and material strivings are little more than expressions of our late-modern denial of death – our clinging to a certainty and permanence we will never find in this life. In our seeking of immortality just as in our fearful clinging to those things we hold most dear – even something as seemingly pure as the safety of an innocent child – we reveal our preference to preserve (again, our belief in the rational) instead of to risk in faith.

pDan: The other counterweight here is a rejection of the assumption that working for IJM is inherently "mission" or even inherently "Christian." It can be, but it need not be. There are surely folks working in such a capacity for the thrill of it all and the career advancement found in such esteemed environs. Further, you aren't disciples of the gospel of Western notions of criminal justice, but the gospel of Shalom. Taken on the whole though, the life of Jake y Rachel is telling a particular story about the world and God's role in it; it whispers of Christ doing "a new thing" in creation. I think you are about that story, about that creation. If that's even remotely true, then there is a missional component to your charge. It will suffice.

pDan is one of those rare, truly good friends. He knows me well. He knows in these words that he is challenging me to ensure they are true – that I am not going back out there for some deluded belief in the ultimate good of IJM's model or the thrill or self-promotion or whatever self-actualizing end I might be pursuing today. And, of course, on some level, I am and always will be off on such misguided quests. But, in many ways, this time feels different.

pDan: While this decision is not about legacy in the self-serving sense, it is about legacy in terms of what story it is that you're telling your children. Your life and the particular way it was lived is the only

*story you really get to convincingly tell. This haunts me daily. I can
tell my daughter and soon-to-be-here child all day about the injustices
in the world and our role in remedying them, but the content of
my speech will always pale in comparison to the form of life I bear
witness to. Under no circumstances does one need to go to Cambodia
to experience or enact a Christ-centered form of life, but one does not
happen upon such a form of life accidentally. It is built of a litany of
small decisions, all of which form a mosaic for your children about
the telos of life. You cannot really give them anything better or more
potent.*

As I weigh the costs of these last years moving, living, and
raising a daughter overseas during a pandemic, this is the part
which ushers in the most hope. My wander-lost life – the antics,
the adventures, the ambitions, all of it – has undoubtedly been
in various ways about legacy formation in the vein of Achilles.
With the birth of my daughter all of that seemed to fade away,
almost in an instant. I now see the true task of my life to be
the "telling of a story of what happened to me," as Carse says,
for her. If I cannot do that, then, in many ways "nothing has
happened at all."

The story my life tells *for her* today from Phnom Penh cannot
help on many levels but be a good one. As she begins her own
story, I cannot think of a better community for her to witness.
Exactly as you might imagine if you know the story of this
organization, the women and men of IJM Cambodia loom large
as the kind of modern heroes of the faith I hope she might one
day aim to emulate. Theirs, if not quite mine, is a story which
beckons her to steadfastly, even at risk to her own life, seek
justice for and solidarity with the vulnerable while leaning
deeply into that great adventure we call love.

*pDan: In thinking about this extraordinary opportunity before you
– and it is truly extraordinary – I'm struck by my own feeling of levity
regarding this decision. Yes, it's easy for me to light about this given
no one has asked me to leave all I've known and loved and fly headlong*

into the blazing unknown. But I'm struck by how I don't think either of you have to be afraid. It's a serious decision, yes. Deadly serious. But you need not be afraid. Please remember that. You need not be afraid. And at the end of the day, you can always ask yourself the age-old question, "why not be utterly changed into fire?"

* * *

Several years on from pDan's epic tome of an email and we aren't yet "utterly changed into fire." But here we are, reasonably at peace with a path which led us and a newborn to the other side of the world in the middle of a pandemic immediately after I'd drafted a book about the ills of travel.

So, then again, maybe we are heading in that direction.

* * *

It was around Evie's first birthday — some months back now — when the fires of COVID and Cambodia felt like they might just consume me. The year passed in but a moment for our young US passport holder. She laughed and cried and ate and slept, basking in the ephemerality of each moment as the sunlight fell softly through her nursery window.

Though we were and are still relatively new in this place, I too felt a bit as if I'd spent the majority of my conscious life in this foreign metropolis.

The task of building a life in a new city – in a new country – in the middle of a pandemic is undeniably hard. Though, after all these years, I still so easily forget that hard isn't necessarily the same as bad.

The baby is healthy and joyful. Rachel has found good, flexible work as a therapist. We are making friends, forging the tiniest little roots of community in the steaming, locked-down, foreign, concrete jungle we now call home.

In another year, these shaky hands – now twitching as they do for a new adventure when life slips into a predictable mold – might take advantage of cheap, regional flights and jet off to an island or drive up a windy mountain pass, or get out of this city, out of my apartment for goodness sakes, anywhere, just go.

But it is not another year. It is this one, this in-between time. And so I wait alongside the rest of the world.

As I end my tale, I ask myself, what are we to do with such moments? What of the days spent waiting? What do we do, when we're stuck inside with limited access to our material distractions and new destinations to see and conquer and post about, hoping others might notice? How might we become something different, something healthier, something better postured toward our true longings?

Instead of escapist fantasies or ruminations on opportunities lost or goals left collecting dust in the wake of an unexpected global and personal tragedy, maybe now is the time to lean down and kiss that baby who is smiling there, naive to the world burning around her as the sunlight falls softly on her head. For once, there is no pressure to be elsewhere. Indeed, there is nowhere else to be but here in this in-between moment with her.

Or, stated differently, maybe now is the time to summon those last vestiges of perseverance and bits of character we thought left us long ago and "fly headlong into the blazing unknown."

* * *

This time, for me, that "blazing unknown" is no longer a physical manifestation of my desire to be something more than myself – the wind in my face in some metaphysical truck bed. This time, it is that halting, doubting, still totally non-linear journey of surrender to our "fundamentally Other" God who once became human and remains in solidarity with our wander-lost yearnings and ceaseless striving and endless internal turmoil.

Indeed, He is with us in this and all unique and trying times of fatigue and weariness and doubt and eagerness to move beyond the challenge at hand. He beckons us even now into His arms, into the terrifying risk and grand adventure of practicing our faith and hope and love amidst the beautiful shipwreck of life, these sacred moments of expectation.

Acknowledgements

It turns out writing a book is a major team effort and I'm immensely grateful for mine. Thank you to all those who read and provided helpful feedback to early versions of the manuscript – Rachel Sims, Dan Hoffman, Jess Mittleman, Brant Copen, Dave Eubank, Aaron Griffith, Dean Sims, Elizabeth Sims, Ethan Harrison, Lauren Harrison, Elizabeth Trotter, and David Kopp. Your time and patience and kind but firm words strengthened this project tremendously and brought me to a place of relative peace about sending my first book out to the real world.

Enormous thanks to McGregor & Luedeke Literary Agency for seeing potential in me and the project at an early stage. Particular gratitude is due Amanda Luedeke for her encouragement, camaraderie, and excellent representation throughout. I can't imagine a better guide into the literary world. And, of course, thank you to Dominic James and John Hunt Publishing for taking a chance on a new author and a risky genre. Here's hoping it was a good bet.

A book about community would be incomplete without explicit acknowledgment of those communities which formed its various inflection points. My life has benefitted richly from intersection with extraordinary individuals and my story would be incomplete without them.

For *Section 2: Young Achilles,* I want to first thank my parents, Dean and Elizabeth Sims, for loving me well; believing in me (perhaps beyond merit); and doing their best to instill something resembling character into a wild and impetuous child. I don't live it perfectly, but I *know* beyond doubt what it looks like to love my own family well because I saw them do it first. This is perhaps the most lasting gift a parent can offer. Unbeknownst to Young Achilles, Joseph and Diane Duarte were simultaneously offering the same to their young daughter just a few hundred miles north. For this and a later invitation to join the family, I am eternally indebted.

I also want to thank my sister, Sarah, for being my first friend and stalwart childhood companion. Our simple days of imaginative play, pop-tart smuggling, and late-night walkie talkie comms are the happiest memories from my childhood. That these fun times facilitated a relationship with someone I still respect, admire and love talking to about all manner of subjects is a great blessing indeed.

Though their names aren't mentioned directly, my childhood buddies Jason Rutherford and Caleb Davison were and continue to be faithful friends and are just the sort of folk who will challenge you to be the best version of yourself.

The amorphous "crew" of *Section 3: On college* picked up right on cue as L flung myself into that oh-so-classically-American moment of rebirth. To my Zerbe, Zenoid, Latvian, and Palace roomates/hall mates, it was a wild ride but a true gift living and growing and getting into trouble with you. To the AOs, I can only wonder/shudder at what might have been. I'm sorry for breaking your hearts in rejection even though I was undeniably born to be one of you. That I count so many of you among my dearest friends today just makes me giddy. And to my other friends – "To Bill" and the Okies, Rugby, Frisbee, Cross Country, RAs, and the "generally unaffiliated" – thank you each for your lasting influence during and beyond those crazy years.

I owe deep gratitude to the women and men of International Justice Mission and Compassion International who mentored and befriended me during my earliest forays into the field of global development, amongst others: Lauren Weaver, Sean Litton, Gary Haugen, Jim Martin, Austin Graff, Betsy Hutson, Deb Rusch, Chris Delvaille, and Russ Debenport. I owe an equivalent debt to my intern cohorts those two summers whose sheer impressiveness catalyzed my nascent journeys toward personal humility and vocation.

As I embarked on *Section 4: On exploration* two names in particular are owed a profound debt. Dave Eubank (Founder, Free Burma Rangers) and Matthew Bugher (formerly of Harvard Human Rights Clinic) welcomed me into their work, introducing a deeply unqualified individual to the esteemed worlds of humanitarian intervention and international human rights law. If my eyes were opened in college, my first stint in Southeast Asia put me on a path from which there was no return. To the many other friends and colleagues which made that experience uniquely formative, thank you. Amongst many others: Oliver Crocco, John Briggs, Jens Lindberg, Micah Beckwith, Zhang Sao, Monkey, Esther & Gaux, Sin, Marika, Ekk Jampa, Oi, Benz, Shani, the list goes on.

In London, I am supremely thankful for intellectual kindred spirits like the brilliant Matheus Ortega, Michael Monroe, and Adil Garane as well as to the faculty at LSE and beyond who guided and mentored me including: Stewart Gordon, Tim Allen, Paul Collier, and the late great David Graeber. And most importantly, to my excellent roommates, all of whom I now count as lifelong friends: Ben Johnson, Jonathan Crowe, and Jed Bartlett – also to Matt and Patty Bolian who graciously hosted me many-a-night in their Westminster flat. To my brother Willy and the children of Busia, thank you for allowing me to play a small part in your story.

In *Section 5: Together* the list grows ever-wider and the debts more deeply felt as time is still not so long past. To the many friends from the road – traveling with BMC, WWInc., and AidData to the far-flung reaches of the planet – I am forever changed by my growing appreciation of the massive, beautiful cultural and intellectual diversity afforded this world.

To the Olivero Farm, we love you. Don't give up on us. We are coming home someday. Though, with your new Peloton-enhanced fitness, you may no longer wish to hike with us when that day dawns.

For the rekindling of old college friends in DC and the birth of FriendsGiving, I am immensely grateful. If for no other reason: an annual excuse to re-assert my marginal athletic abilities over an underwhelming group of washed-up jokester-jocks is deeply gratifying (Klossy, I'm looking at you). The knowledge that we can come back inside with our broken bodies and immediately connect on the deepest of levels (plus fart jokes) is one of my life's great joys. Especial gratitude to Shane and Julie Murphy from this group for their faithful friendship and travel companionship over the years; their unmatched ability to host; and for proving to me and the world that it is indeed possible to have children and simultaneously be mad cool.

To JART, you are our hart (er, heart). We love you and miss you like the sun misses the flower.

And to the folks who endured me at W&M, I guess you are okay as well. Thanks to Mike Tierney for letting me join the wild experiment in cross-disciplinary student-faculty collaboration, beer, and, occasionally, research that is GRI. HHH-HyperCore thank you for begrudgingly incorporating my "alternate narratives" into your weird clique of counter-PC, post-structuralist, cynical anti-establishmentarian dysphoria. Thanks to Ethan Harrison, Christian Baehr, Bryan Burgess, and Juju Pepe for indulging my last, beautiful moment in the sun pretending I was still in college. Well, I guess Mike is still doing it, so who knows.

To the insanity that is DHMH, thank you for welcoming me into the most meaningful and, somehow, simultaneously, frivolous community I've ever encountered. With Jeremy's passing, the core of my community of kindred spirits died as well. Being in your midst keeps his memory alive for me and, equally important, ushers me into that sacred land of the kind of deep, committed friendships which are too rare in this day. To do this, to be so effortlessly there for one another, and to invite me to witness and even participate in a small way is the most healing gift I could ever have received in the wake of a great personal tragedy. That you embody this all on epic hikes of questionable judgment or sanity and in *causa sui* pursuit of silly mishaps just goes to show that God has a terrific sense of humor and irony.

To Allison Hoffman, thank you for being the godmother to our daughter and the actual, literal soul-mate to my intellectual soulmate. pDan, you are one of a kind. The world needs more of you and since it is unlikely to get that, it needs to hear your voice. Will it matter in the grand story of the cosmos? No, probably not, but it will be beautiful. And sure, we'll get you some pseudonyms as convincing as Kierkegaards'. Get writing my friend.

To Gary Haugen and the IJM Family, thanks for having me back. To Andrey Sawchenko, thanks for showing me what it looks like to be a truly excellent leader. And to the women and men of IJM Cambodia, thanks for being the most inspiring team I've ever had the pleasure to serve.

Lastly, to Rachel, this book and the tattered life behind it are the best excuse for a love letter I can muster. This journey – the wandering lostness of it all – is worth undertaking for me because of you. Thank you for showing me daily the best witness of love I could ever hope to encounter and, in so doing, pointing me back to the Source of that Love.

Thank you all the more for loving our precious daughter so well and so selflessly. The rest of this journey, together is a story of three (or perhaps more). EvieBaby, you are my life. From here, at "the pinnacle," with all the advantages and crutches and beautiful friendships I could ever ask for, I only pray for the character to live a story worth telling, for you.

Author Bio

J. Daniel Sims serves as Director of IJM Cambodia where he leads a team of investigators, lawyers, social workers, programmatic, and operational staff in the fight against labor exploitation. Concurrently with his role at IJM, he serves as a Non-Resident Fellow at Duke University's Center for Reconciliation, a leading institute bridging the worlds of research and practice in the global peace-building and justice space. Sims previously directed international development policy research and taught courses at the College of William & Mary, led humanitarian programs in northern Myanmar, and co-founded a social justice organization in eastern Uganda. He is happily married to his best friend, Rachel, and is the proud papa of the cutest baby on the planet.

The Scarlet Cord
Conversations With God's Chosen Women
Lindsay Hardin Freeman, Karen N. Canton
Voiceless wax figures no longer, twelve biblical women,
outspoken, independent, faithful, selfless risk-takers, come to life
in *The Scarlet Cord*.
Paperback: 978-1-84694-375-1

Will You Join in Our Crusade?
The Invitation of the Gospels Unlocked by the Inspiration of
Les Miserables
Steve Mann
Les Miserables' narrative is entwined with Bible study in this book
of 42 daily readings from the Gospels, perfect for Lent or anytime.
Paperback: 978-1-78279-384-7 ebook: 978-1-78279-383-0

A Quiet Mind
Uniting Body, Mind and Emotions in Christian Spirituality
Eva McIntyre
A practical guide to finding peace in the present moment that will
change your life, heal your wounds and bring you a quiet mind.
Paperback: 978-1-84694-507-6 ebook: 978-1-78099-005-7

Readers of ebooks can buy or view any of these bestsellers by
clicking on the live link in the title. Most titles are published in
paperback and as an ebook. Paperbacks are available in traditional
bookshops. Both print and ebook formats are available online.

Find more titles and sign up to our readers' newsletter at http://
www.johnhuntpublishing.com/christianity. Follow us on Facebook
at https://www.facebook.com/ChristianAlternative.

The Long Road to Heaven,
A Lent Course Based on the Film
Tim Heaton
This second Lent resource from the author of *The Naturalist and the Christ* explores Christian understandings of "salvation" in a five-part study based on the film *The Way*.
Paperback: 978-1-78279-274-1 ebook: 978-1-78279-273-4

Abide In My Love
More Divine Help for Today's Needs
John Woolley
The companion to *I Am With You, Abide In My Love* offers words of divine encouragement.
Paperback: 978-1-84694-276-1

From the Bottom of the Pond
The Forgotten Art of Experiencing God in the Depths of the Present Moment
Simon Small
From the Bottom of the Pond takes us into the depths of the present moment, to the only place where God can be found.
Paperback: 978-1-84694-066-8 ebook: 978-1-78099-207-5

God Is A Symbol Of Something True
Why You Don't Have to Choose Either a Literal Creator God or a Blind, Indifferent Universe
Jack Call
In this examination of modern spiritual dilemmas, Call offers the explanation that some of the most important elements of life are beyond our control: everything is fundamentally alright.
Paperback: 978-1-84694-244-0

CIRCLE
BOOKS

CHRISTIAN FAITH

Circle Books explores a wide range of disciplines within the field of Christian faith and practice. It also draws on personal testimony and new ways of finding and expressing God's presence in the world today.

If you have enjoyed this book, why not tell other readers by posting a review on your preferred book site. Recent bestsellers from Circle Books are:

I Am With You (Paperback)
John Woolley

These words of divine encouragement were given to John Woolley in his work as a hospital chaplain, and have since inspired and uplifted tens of thousands, even changed their lives.
Paperback: 978-1-90381-699-8 ebook: 978-1-78099-485-7

God Calling
A. J. Russell

365 messages of encouragement channelled from Christ to two anonymous "Listeners".
Hardcover: 978-1-905047-42-0 ebook: 978-1-78099-486-4

Note to Reader

Dear Reader,

Thank you for purchasing *WanderLOST*. My sincere hope is that you derived as much from engaging with this project as I did in creating it. If you have a few moments, please feel free to add your review of the book at your favorite online site for feedback. Also, if you would like to connect with other books that I have coming in the near future, please visit my website for news on upcoming works, recent blog posts and to sign up for my newsletter.

Sincerely,

Jake

Twitter: @jdanielsims

Linkedin: jacobsims1